Appointment in Rome

Appointment in Rome

The Church in America Awakening

Richard John Neuhaus

A Herder and Herder Book
The Crossroad Publishing Company
New York

The Crossroad Publishing Company
370 Lexington Avenue, New York, NY 10017

Printed in the United States of America

Library of Congress Cataloging-in-Publication Data

Neuhaus, Richard John.
    Appointment in Rome : the Church in America awakening / Richard
John Neuhaus.
        p.   cm.
    "A Herder and Herder book."
    Includes bibliographical references.
    ISBN 0-8245-1555-2
    1. Catholic Church—America—History—20th century.   2. Catholic
Church—America—Congresses.   3. Synod for America (1997 : Rome,
Italy)   I. Title
    BX1401.N48   1999
    282'.7'09049—dc21   98-37349
                                                          CIP

For Avery Dulles, S.J.,

on his eightieth birthday

Friend, Mentor, and Exemplary Theologian
of the Church

Contents

Acknowledgments

I AM INDEBTED, FIRST, to the bishops and other participants in the synod, many of whom I counted as friends before the event and many more after. Then to George Weigel, who has been a fellow traveler on so many journeys, and to his wife, Joan, whose helpfulness knows no bounds. To Father Tom Williams of the Legionaries of Christ for his translating, transporting, and generous readiness to assist. To Bishop James Harvey, Prefect of the Pontifical Household, for sterling company and invaluable counsel. To Monsignor Timothy Dolan, Rector of the North American College, and to the college's students and faculty, for their hospitality and invariable kindness. Others will, I trust, recognize their contribution to this book. All are responsible for whatever may be its merits. As for its failings, I can only say I did my best.

A Word to the Reader

T HIS BOOK IS, ABOVE ALL, a story. It is, most immediately, the story
of what happened when Pope John Paul II called together several
hundred bishops and other Catholic leaders (the latter term is loosely
defined) to join him in thinking about the past and the future of the
Church in America—"America" meaning here North, Central, South,
and the Caribbean. The official name of this appointment in Rome is
the Special Assembly for America of the Synod of Bishops. But it is
commonly called the Synod for America.

It is hard to say when this story begins. We could date it from two
thousand years ago when, as Christians believe, God became man in
Jesus Christ. Since the synod is one event among countless others in
the ongoing life of the Church, we could say the story begins with the
outpouring of the Holy Spirit on Pentecost, often called the birthday
of the Church. Or an argument could be made for going back almost
two thousand years before that, to when God called Abraham from Ur
of the Chaldeans and made him, as Catholics say in the Mass, our
"father in faith"—and father of the elect people from whom would
come the Savior of the world. Pushing the point farther, others might
insist that our story begins in creation with the majestic announcement
of Genesis, "In the beginning God created the heavens and the earth."
That may appear to be reaching, but it is of the utmost importance, I
believe, to see this Synod for America within the big picture of what is
called the story of salvation. It is not a freestanding event that can be
understood apart from that big picture.

It is also, of course, a story that fits the category of current affairs.
The goings-on inside the Vatican are endlessly fascinating. Journalists

delight in writing titillating reports about what are inevitably called the "intrigues" taking place within the Roman Curia, which is the bureaucracy that assists the pope in governing a universal Church of more than one billion members. The Curia makes for inviting journalistic copy because it is composed of congregations, councils, and other offices (the main parts of the Curia are known as "dicasteries") which are depicted as very old, very secretive, and very given to conspiracy. Then there are those cardinals, bishops, and monsignori all dressed up and furtively going to and fro amidst brightly arrayed Swiss Guards, on business about which the world can only speculate. The whole thing is, as they say, exceedingly "colorful." It helps also that the Catholic Church is the world's most enduring and largest institution.

The story told in the following pages may have the effect of "demystifying" the everyday reality of the Vatican, and that might be all to the good. But I hope the story does not detract from the deeper mystery of which this Synod for America is part. "Mystery" here does not refer to a puzzlement—as in a mystery novel—but to the often elusive ways in which God works his purposes through time. The more immediate history that frames the context of our story begins with the Second Vatican Council, which was convened by Pope John XXIII in 1962 and concluded by Pope Paul VI in 1965. The present pope views the council as opening a new chapter in the history of the Church and of the world. He views his pontificate, which began in 1978, as a continuation of that chapter, the purpose of which is to prepare the Church and the world for what he has called a "springtime of renewal" at the beginning of the third Christian millennium. This note of preparation and of heightened expectation, he has said, is the "hermeneutical key" to his pontificate. It is also the key to understanding the Synod for America.

In 1994, John Paul II issued an apostolic letter that is titled *Tertio Millennio Adveniente* ("As the Third Millennium Nears"). In that letter, he called for the convening of continental synods of the worldwide Church—synods for Africa, Europe, Asia, Oceania, and America (meaning all the Americas). The American hemisphere includes half the Catholics in the world and, as we shall see, deliberating about a phenomenon so vast and various is a cumbersome process. It is frequently a contentious process as well. At the same time, it is not without its moments of inspiration and even comic relief. Looking back on that month in Rome, I am not entirely sure what it accomplished. The pope pronounced himself more than pleased with the exercise, and it is his judgment that matters most.

What you have here is an unofficial—a *very* unofficial—report on what happened at the Synod for America, and what it might mean for the future of the Catholic Church and of the larger Christian movement in places as different as Caracas and Quebec, Chicago and Havana, Mexico City and Worcester, Massachusetts. Through the meetings and speeches and arguments that surround the drafting and redrafting of documents and that inform the interplay of politics and personalities is the awareness that something great, something both ominous and promising, is afoot. To be sure, there are also routine, and repetition, and weariness, and moments bordering on the silly. But at the end of the day, the story of the Synod for America is part of the story of a Church and a world being put on alert to *Tertio Millennio Adveniente*, a springtime of renewal. If we have the nerve for it. If we have the wit for it. If we have the faith for it.

Richard John Neuhaus
New York, New York

1

Mostly Christian America

How the Synod Happened and What It Hopes to Do

NOT SINCE THAT YEAR in the fourth grade under Miss Woodward have I experienced such tedium. Please do not misunderstand. I was not indifferent to the honor when I received the message that Pope John Paul II had appointed me a member of the Special Assembly for America of the Synod of Bishops. For one thing, I am not even a bishop. There are four others from among the unmitred who were also appointed members of this assembly and thus designated "synod fathers" along with cardinals, curial prefects, presidents of pontifical dicasteries, archbishops, and bishops gathered from the frozen tundra of Canada to the southernmost tip of Chile, or, as it is repeatedly said here, "from Alaska to Tierra del Fuego." There are 297 participants in the synod, of whom 233 of us are synod fathers with the right to vote.

The other nonbishops who are synod fathers hold important posts in the larger scheme of things. There are the general secretaries of the bishops' conferences in the United States and Canada, for instance, and Father Marcial Maciel, founder and superior general of the Legionaries of Christ, a vibrant renewal movement of hundreds of priests and seminarians in Europe and the Americas. And nobody would question the inclusion of the father general of the Jesuits, often (although less frequently in recent years) called "the black pope," Peter-Hans Kolvenbach.

What I am doing here has not been explained to me. To expect an explanation, I am told by those with more experience in the ways of Rome, is an American habit that is not to be indulged. The Roman way of communication leans heavily on what is called indirection. The story is told of two curial cardinals walking down the street and getting caught in a downpour. They seek refuge from the deluge by huddling in a doorway. The one says, "It appears it might rain." The other responds, "So they say."

As best I can tell, I am here because I'm supposed to know something about the state of the Church in America, and especially about Catholic relations with other religious groups, such as the evangelical Protestants whom our Latin American brothers are inclined to deride as "the sects." On that subject more in due course. In any event, here I am sitting with Father Maciel on my left and Father Kolvenbach on my right, in our plain black cassocks amid a splendid display of cardinal red and episcopal purple. Here we all are, hour after tedious hour, relieved in part by the fact that there, right there in front of us, sits the pope, hour after tedious hour. If he can take it, who are we to complain? I remember the telephone call from the papal nuncio in Washington saying that the Holy Father wanted me in Rome from November 16 through December 12. I didn't think I could say that I didn't have time.

The pope obviously thinks this is important. In frail physical health, at an age much more advanced than mine, and with duties immeasurably more pressing, the pope takes time for this. Every day when the synod gathers in general session, he is there; from nine to half past noon and then back again for another session from five to seven o'clock in the evening; there at the head of the class he patiently sits listening to literally hundreds of speeches. Surely he has heard all this before. He hardly lacks opportunities for listening to bishops. Since the start of his pontificate in 1978, John Paul II has riled curial habits by greatly extending the time he spends with bishops who come from all over the world to make their *ad limina* visits every five years. Thousands of bishops have had his ear now for almost twenty years. Moreover, each day he has groups of synod fathers in for lunch and dinner, and listens again. Nonetheless, there he sits and listens, and listens, and listens. To be sure, he nods from time to time, and sometimes seems to be reading a book or saying his prayers. (Most everybody nods from time to time, an indulgence encouraged by endless speeches, plus the warm temperature and poor air circulation in the synod hall, here called the "aula.")

If the pope thinks this synod business is so very important, as he obviously does, and if one believes that he is, not to put too fine a point

on it, the apostle Peter among us, as I sincerely do, attention must be paid. But one cannot help thinking the process need not be so boring. The cultivation of patience is good for the soul, I tell myself, and I mostly believe it. But to paraphrase Lincoln on the fellow ridden out of town on a rail—if it weren't for the honor of the thing, I would just as soon be taking care of business back in New York. The last resort when faced by the prospect of unavoidable exasperation is to say it is "a learning experience," and the synod certainly is that.

Patience is to be learned, and perhaps just a touch of humility. On the long list of synod fathers (called the *Elenchus Participantium*), I note that my name appears dead last. I realize I am not accustomed to that back in my little world among the many worlds of New York City. But this is Rome. Eternal Rome, the center of the one, holy, catholic, and apostolic Church, or at least, as Catholics believe, the center of that Church most fully and rightly ordered through time. I survey all these cardinals, archbishops, and bishops. The ones who are not permanently ensconced here in Rome must be thinking about all they could be doing back home. I rather hope they are thinking that, although I suppose some are glad to get away for a month, and a few might even be pondering the attractions of a permanent appointment here at the center of things.

An Experiment in "Collegiality"

The idea of a Synod for America is something new. Such a thing has never happened before. For the purposes of the synod, "America" is very emphatically in the singular, and it includes North, South, Central, the Caribbean, and the whole continental shebang. The idea of a synod is not quite so new. In fact, it goes back to the early centuries of the Church when bishops of a region would get together to sort out their problems and decide on common approaches for the future. The word "synod" comes from the Greek for "walking together" and is mainly a matter of sitting together and talking together and praying together until we discern a way of walking together.

The Synod of Bishops in its present form is a permanent institution established by Pope Paul VI following the Second Vatican Council. At the council, which concluded in 1965 on a note of high euphoria, bish-

ops from around the world were much taken with the idea of "collegiality." Collegiality meant that the universal Church would no longer be governed by ukases from Rome Central. Rather, the pope would govern in institutionalized consultation with the bishops. A good many bishops who were much taken with "the spirit" of Vatican II went far beyond the letter of the council and envisioned a new structure in which the pope would be much like a president in a parliamentary democracy. He would be first among equals, *primus inter pares*, and the permanent synod would be the legislative body where the real decisions are made.

Here at the Synod for America there have been a number of interventions urging that this assembly should become a permanent body for the deliberation of things touching on the Church in the Americas. Older hands tell me this is par for the course in such synod assemblies, reflecting a vestigial longing for that older idea of "collegiality" in which the papal office would give way to a system of power sharing. Of course this is the Church, and nobody speaks of power in such crude terms. An American archbishop tells me: "I've been to most of these synods, and every time there are voices raised for the revolution that was not to be. The idea that collegiality means democracy dies hard."

The *Vademecum Synodi*, or handbook, that is handed out at the start of the synod leaves no doubt about the extent and limit of our authority. "By its nature, the Synod of Bishops has the task of giving advice and counsel. Therefore, its recommendations are reserved exclusively to the Supreme Pontiff." The permanent institution is the Synod of Bishops, which is run by a Vatican office headed by His Eminence Jan Cardinal Schotte, a Belgian who, as is said, runs a tight ship. The idea of a permanent Synod of Bishops is instantiated, so to speak, by fairly regular gatherings of bishops to offer the pope "advice and counsel" on specified questions. Under Paul VI and John Paul II, such assemblies have happened every two or three years, taking up questions as various as evangelization, priestly formation, the Christian family, and the consecrated life of religious orders. Whatever one's dissatisfactions with the way the synod is run, it is worth keeping in mind that it is only a twenty-five-year-old institution in a Church that is two thousand years old. As an institution, it is still finding its way. It is not a legislative assembly, nor is it merely a sounding board for the pope. Maybe it is something in between, or maybe it will turn out to be a third thing

altogether. Whatever else it is, it is a continuing experiment in giving flesh to the council's affirmation of collegiality.

As the Third Millennium Nears

The Synod for America is different from earlier synods in several ways, not least being that the agenda seems to be wide open. When the process got under way more than two years ago, Cardinal Schotte's office proposed to the bishops some questions for deliberation, but everything that touches on the present problems and future prospects of the Church in the Western Hemisphere was fair game. The idea of such a synod was first raised by the pope at a meeting of the Latin American episcopate in October 1992. Later he issued an apostolic letter, *Tertio Millennio Adveniente* ("As the Third Millennium Nears"), in which the idea had grown to invoking synods that would include the whole world. The Synod for Africa has already been held; Europe, Asia, Oceania, and wherever else the Church is to be found will soon get their turns. Now America is at bat, a continent that includes, we are regularly reminded, about one-half of the billion Catholics in the world today.

The idea of *Tertio Millennio Adveniente* is, as the title suggests, to get the Church and the world ready for the third Christian millennium. The world has learned to count by Christian time, but that doesn't mean that the world will observe the turn of the millennium in a Christian way. One New York travel-and-entertainment conglomerate is taking reservations for grand millennium bashes on December 31, 1999, in New York, London, Prague, Tokyo, Rio de Janeiro, and Paris. The organizers of millennium parties for the jet set did not include Bethlehem or Jerusalem on the itinerary. Why drag religion into the business of observing the millennium? It is no secret, however, that the pope earnestly wants to visit the Holy Land during the millennium year, but whether political circumstances there will make that possible is very much in doubt. He has declared the year 2000 a Jubilee Year, and it is expected that mass pilgrimages to Rome will turn the traffic and logistics of this city into whatever is on the far side of its routine anarchy.

One regularly hears from the pedants who tell us that the pope and everybody else got the date wrong. Don't they know that the best of scholarship suggests that Jesus of Nazareth was born in what we reckon as the year 6 B.C., and therefore we entered the third millennium in 1995? Alternatively, we are told that the second millennium ends with the conclusion of the year 2000, and therefore the beginning of the third millennium should be observed as January 1, 2001. Of course the pope knows all that perfectly well. One answer is that we are dealing here with the symbolic, and the year 2000 is the number of symbolic force. Another answer is that the whole idea is to get ready for the new millennium, and what better way to do that than to concentrate the mind and soul in the year before it actually arrives?

This Synod for America takes place within the ambiance of the symbolic. I have to keep telling myself that, for it helps temper impatience with the tedium, the repetition, the apparently wasted time. Synod fathers tell me that the event is comparable to a huge transnational corporation bringing together its top management to plan strategy for the future, but that makes no sense at all. A corporation that ran a meeting the way this is run would soon be filing for bankruptcy. That is not, at least not necessarily, a criticism of the synod, which is an essentially different kind of event. In a noteworthy intervention, the feisty young archbishop of Denver, Charles Chaput, poses the question whether the synod fathers view themselves as pastors or managers, shepherds or executives. Whatever role their executive duties compel them to play from day to day back home, and however much they may from time to time be seduced by that role, most of these men obviously do not want to think of themselves as the top management of the Catholic Church, Inc.

The seemingly interminable listening, the convoluted consideration and reconsideration of reconsiderations—all this is not unrelated, I would like to suppose, to what the Bible means by "waiting on the Lord." This enterprise is his, and even those who strut most self-importantly when receiving the snappy salutes that the Swiss Guards bestow upon the princes of the Church seem to know that. The cardinals, the nobility of the Curia, sundry prelates, and the pope himself—all are dressed up for what they know are their passing parts in a party that will look pretty silly if it does not finally culminate in the eschatological Feast of the Lamb. Along the way to that hoped-for consummation, prelates fret about budgets, personnel, promotions, and career paths, just as other managers do. And no doubt some are taken in by the present splendor, being so preoccupied with the management of the provisional moment that they forget the destination.

Over drinks last night, a longtime observer of the Roman scene opined, "These are churchmen. They don't know anything other than the Church." He meant it as a compliment, but I hope he is wrong. It is surely necessary to know the other worlds that the very different world of the Church is called to serve.

Organizing the Synod

The synod starts out with a theme: "Encounter with the Living Jesus Christ: The Way to Conversion, Communion, and Solidarity in America." Day after day, in more than two hundred speeches, that theme will become the synodical argot for proposals on everything from international debt to priestly vocations to respecting the cultures of indigenous peoples. After a while, one can anticipate exactly when an intervention will be clinched by appeal to conversion, communion, or solidarity—especially communion, and most especially solidarity. Not that Jesus Christ does not get a fair number of mentions, but as Joseph Cardinal Ratzinger of the Congregation of the Doctrine of the Faith has occasion to point out, it sometimes does seem that Christ is instrumental to the achievement of other good things, such as solidarity.

It is odd the way this term "solidarity" has caught on. One factor is the Polish labor union of that name, which was so strongly supported by John Paul II in the 1980s and played a crucial part in the beginning of the end of the evil empire of Soviet Communism. But I expect Archbishop Paul Josef Cordes, president of the Pontifical Council "Cor Unum," has a point when he cautions against overreliance on the term. "Solidarity," he says, has a history among anti-Catholic European intellectuals who were quite explicitly looking for a substitute for the Christian language of "charity." Also among politicized Christians of recent decades, "charity" has fallen into disfavor. The answer to the world's problems is not charity but justice, a generation was taught to say. Charity, however, is but another word for love, and the ultimate truth in the Christian scheme of things is that "God is love." These considerations crop up throughout the synod's discussions, evoking reflection on whether, as some say, the old Marxist-oriented liberation theology of the 1970s and 1980s is dead or has simply found different expression in the language of solidarity. It becomes evident that that question is very much on the minds of a number of synod fathers.

The theme—"Encounter with the Living Jesus Christ: The Way to Conversion, Communion, and Solidarity"—was framed by Cardinal Schotte, general secretary of the Synod of Bishops. The assemblies of the synod are very much Schotte's show, and he is obviously a man not intimidated by the charge of heavy-handedness. He sits facing the synod fathers, along with the deputy presidents—since the pope is the president, they are called *praesides delegati*—and the chief secretaries of the synod. Schotte has his chair at the Holy Father's left hand but is clearly his right-hand man in directing the affair. A big and somewhat burly man, he brooks no nonsense. The other morning he made a verbal slip, referring to how the synod is "orchestrated." Quickly catching himself, he smiled and said that he of course meant "organized." One may be permitted to wonder whether he did not have it mostly right the first time.

The organization begins with the announcement that there is going to be a synod. The bishops' conferences in all the countries of America, North and South, are asked what they think are the questions that most need to be addressed. Then Schotte and his aides produce the *Lineamenta*, a kind of preparatory outline that was released in September 1996. This, in turn, is circulated among the national conferences and local churches, and the responses go into the production of the *Instrumentum Laboris*, which is Latin for "working paper." That is the document with which the synod actually gets under way.

I note that Latin figures chiefly in the official nomenclature and in the daily prayers of the synod. Along with Spanish, English, Portuguese, French, and Italian, it is an official language of the synod. But, despite an invitation to do so, nobody makes a speech in Latin, and when it comes to dividing up into language groups for more informal discussions, Latin has no takers. Traditionalist Catholics of a certain bent might be disappointed with that, but will be pleased to know that, later on, when we get to the "propositions" to be offered to the pope, they are all presented in Latin. The reason given is that, if they were written in the other official languages, there would be endless argument over the accuracy of translations. There are also distinct advantages in the use of a language in which few have confidence enough to engage in extended nit-picking. (When we got into the discussion of the *propositiones* in our smaller group, however, I was happily surprised by how many were more or less accomplished Latinists.)

The big session is called *congregatio generalis*, and these are held in the synod aula, which is one flight up from the huge audience hall built by Paul VI and situated just to the left of St. Peter's basilica as viewed from the square. The aula is actually built into the roof of the audience hall. The audience hall itself, which, in one of his earliest acts as pope, John Paul II named in honor of Paul VI, is chiefly distinguished by being very big, accommodating crowds of seven thousand or more for the pope's Wednesday audiences, at which he delivers extended discourses on sundry aspects of Catholic faith and life. He held audiences while the synod was in session, and it is testimony to the soundproofing that one flight up we did not hear the slightest whisper of the wildly cheering throngs below. Upstairs we are seated in a plain beige room whose four hundred or more black vinyl seats are in rows sloping steeply down to the front. Each seat is equipped with a retractable microphone, and synod fathers remain seated while making their interventions, which no doubt discourages overexcited oratory from disturbing the tranquillity of the proceedings. There are earphones for simultaneous translation from the several official languages, but I note that most of the fathers don't use them, which indicates admirable linguistic facility, or that they are not paying close attention.

The space is more or less identical to lecture rooms that might be found in any American university, except for the big crucifix and the icon of the Madonna and Child above the place where the pope sits, along with Cardinal Schotte and the lower praesidium. Seats are assigned according to the strict protocol of precedence. At the front, immediately facing the pope, are the cardinals—about forty of them, arranged by order of when they received their red hats, or birettas. At the synod the cardinals wear their red zucchettos, which is a skullcap, known to New Yorkers as a yarmulke. Right behind the cardinals are the fraternal delegates (*delegati fraterni*), four ecumenical representatives from the councils of churches in Canada, the United States, and the Caribbean, plus one from the Lutheran church in Brazil. Their presence is an important gesture, and each brings greetings to the synod and gets to speak, although not to vote, in the smaller meetings.

One cannot help but note that there are no representatives from the evangelical and pentecostal groups that are of such particular concern to the Latin Americans. The *delegati fraterni* who are invited can be counted on to be fraternal. Although one of them, George Vandervelde of the Canadian Council of Churches, does not hesitate to point out that the *Instrumentum Laboris* and the synod discussion do not reflect the level of ecumenical urgency that the Church officially professes. He is right, of course. Apart from Latin American anxiety about the invasion of "the sects," allegedly orchestrated by the United States, the existence of other Christians does not weigh heavily on the mind of the synod. As one not unsympathetic bishop remarked during the coffee break, "We got enough to do dealing with the problems of half a billion Catholics. Ecumenism will have to wait." That view is sharply challenged in the synod by Edward Cardinal Cassidy, president of the Pontifical Council for Christian Unity, as it has been challenged over the years by John Paul's persistently repeated ecumenical concern, but one can understand why for many bishops ecumenism is nowhere near the top of their concerns.

Behind the cardinals and fraternal delegates are seated, row upon row, the archbishops and bishops, and behind them the unmitred few among the synod fathers. The maxim of Jesus that the last shall be first will have to await another dispensation. Behind us, up in the bleachers, so to speak, are the *adiutores et adiutrices secretarii specialis*—auditors and experts, lay and clergy, men and women, about sixty in all. The auditors get to speak in general session, although they are allotted only six minutes per intervention, while the synod fathers get all of eight minutes. Theirs are some of the more striking interventions, however. For instance, Mary Ann Glendon of Harvard Law School on healing the breach between conservatives and liberals by bringing the social concerns of "solidarity" into closer conversation with the theology of "communion," and Sister Mary Bernard Nettle of the Council of Major Superiors of Women Religious on "the culture of life" and what that means in caring for the sick and dying. The experts, in addition to enduring the apparently endless sessions, render invaluable service behind the scenes by collating ideas, translating texts, and tempering episcopal pronouncements by reference to pertinent facts.

How Is the Pope?

It is, all in all, an impressive assembly. Here is Francis Cardinal Arinze, a most personable, articulate, and vibrantly orthodox figure with a marvelous sense of humor. He's the curial official in charge of dialogue with other religions. A Nigerian, he is often mentioned as the next pope. "But do you think the Church is ready for a black pope?" an archbishop responds when I mention the possibility. I can hardly think of a stronger statement of the Church's universality, or of a man more capable and holy. Others are mentioned, of course. Rome is filled with Great Mentioners, and the subject of the next pope is a perennial in private conversations. That has always been the case in Rome, even if the current pope had been elected only yesterday. On another occasion, the name of Jean-Marie Cardinal Lustiger, archbishop of Paris, comes up in informal discussion and a synod father, a cardinal, asked, "Do you think the Church is ready for a Jewish pope?"

No doubt twenty years ago there were those who asked, "Do you think the Church is ready for a Polish pope?" Those who seem to doubt that the Church is ready for the untried frequently mention Pio Cardinal Laghi as a possible next pope. A very attractive figure with extensive experience as nuncio in both South and North America, Laghi is prefect of the Congregation for Catholic Education. Against him is his age, since he is not all that much younger than the present pope, and he is Italian. Cardinal Martini of Milan is also much mentioned, but he shares with Laghi the drawbacks of age and nationality, and he is a Jesuit. According to the journalistic wisdom, Martini is the candidate of "the liberals," but it is not at all clear what that means. There is a feeling that the Church is not ready to return to what some view as the Italian captivity of the papacy. In recent pontificates, the college of cardinals has been thoroughly internationalized and Italians are now a relatively small minority. Talk about who is and who is not *papabile*—loosely translated as "popeable"—is endemic. One is regularly reminded of the old saying that a cardinal who goes into the conclave as *papabile* comes out as a cardinal. On the other hand, some go in as *papabile* and come out as pope, which was the case in 1978 when Karol Cardinal Wojtyla came out as Pope John Paul II. (At least among Vatican insiders he was thought to be *papabile*, although the ever-alert press corps was taken completely by surprise.)

Vatican-watchers in the press are engaged in a constant and ghoulish death watch, no matter how healthy a pope may be. Their excuse for their skepticism is that, according to the official statements of the Vatican, a pope is never sick until he is dead. So, they say, their duty is to be constantly watching for any sign of the pope's failing health. Especially in the Italian press, headlines declaring that the pope is near death have become a staple in the last twenty years. And at least once, when Mehemet Ali Agca almost succeeded in assassinating him in May of 1981, the headlines were right. And of course, popes too grow old and weak. Although it is never officially confirmed, a widespread opinion is that John Paul has some form of Parkinson's disease. The physical decline of the last several years is undeniably evident. Medical authorities say the disease follows no certain trajectory.

The Church and the world would likely get used to a spiritually and intellectually vibrant pope who is confined to a wheelchair, just as we have in recent years become accustomed to the cane, the stoop, and the sometimes slurred pronunciation. Here at the synod and in the last few years, I have watched him up close on formal and informal circumstances. In Rome, all eyes are on the pope, for the city gravitates around, derives its very existence from, the man and the office. He looks much better now than when I was last with him a few months ago. He is seventy-eight years old, and I think it likely that he will effectively lead us for years to come. I pray that is the case. On this score, I cannot pretend to be objective. This is one of the most powerful teaching pontificates in the two thousand years of the Church's history, and it has put the leadership of the Church on the world-historical stage in a way that has not happened for centuries.

Now I have wandered from the subject of the Synod for America. But people always ask, How is the pope? Inevitably implicated in that question is another: Who comes next? Moreover, the pope is hardly incidental to the subject of the Synod for America. Apart from the pope, there would be no synod, for it exists solely to give him counsel and advice on what, at the beginning of the third millennium, he should say to and about the Church in America.

Immediately outside the synod aula is a small chapel where the Blessed Sacrament is reserved. It is a room off the corridor along which the pope and the synod fathers enter and leave the hall, except for those of humbler station who are in the upper seats of the hall and use the side stairways to the aula. The thirteen kneelers in the chapel get good use from praying prelates, frequently joined by others kneeling on the floor. One is struck that this is, all in all, a prayerful assembly. It is no little thing that before arriving at the nine o'clock session all the participants have said Morning Prayer and Mass. Then the general sessions begin with the Third Hour (*Hora Tertia*) of the daily office, led by the Holy Father.

Under the Patronage of Our Lady

The Vatican printing office is a wonder, churning out beautifully produced booklets and folders of all kinds for the multitude of events going
on around here. The daily prayer book for the synod is adorned with a
magnificent color print of Our Lady of Guadalupe, a larger rendition
of which is prominently displayed in the chapel. Our Lady of Guadalupe is everywhere encountered in this synod. She is mentioned frequently in interventions by the synod fathers and also figures in the
pope's homilies at the opening and closing Eucharists. The closing
Mass of the synod is on her feast day, December 12. If, as expected, the
pope comes to America to deliver the "exhortation" emerging from this
synod, and if he visits only one city, it will likely be Mexico City at the
basilica shrine of Our Lady of Guadalupe. (Since writing this journal, it
has been announced that the pope will also visit St. Louis, Missouri.)

Devotion to Mary under the title of Our Lady of Guadalupe is often
viewed as mainly a Latin American phenomenon, but she is officially
declared by the Church to be the patroness and mother of all America.
The note is repeatedly struck here that America is composed of many
different peoples. During the synod there will be many interventions
touching on indigenous peoples and their conflicted connections with
the Spanish, who were responsible for "the first evangelization" of
America. The "new evangelization" is a central theme of this pontificate and also of the synod, but it is repeatedly emphasized that the new
evangelization builds on the first evangelization that was launched half
a millennium ago. In his homily at the opening of the synod, John Paul
refers to 1992, "when we solemnly commemorated the five-hundredth
anniversary of the evangelization of America." The year 1992 was a
time when the intellectually fashionable thing was not to solemnly
commemorate but to furiously excoriate the "invasion" of America by
Christopher Columbus and his band of imperialist gangsters.

The pope goes further in his homily: "The fruit of this extraordinary missionary work is the evangelization of America or, as one can
say more precisely, of the 'three Americas,' which today are mostly
Christian. Therefore, it is very important, five centuries later and at the
threshold of the millennium, to mentally review the way taken by
Christianity throughout the whole extent of those lands. It is also
important not to separate the Christian history of North America from
that of Central America and South America. They should be consid-

ered together, safeguarding at the same time the originality of each
one, because they appeared as a single reality to the eyes of those who
reached their shores over five hundred years ago and in particular
because the communion among local communities is a living sign of
that natural unity of the only Church of our Lord Jesus, of which they
are an organic part."

That passage bears close reading. The use of "America" in the singular, as in the Synod for America, is not intended to deny the reality
of the several Americas. Not only the "three" but, as will become evident in the course of the synod, the very different worlds within each.
There is also in the passage a subtle but significant allusion to Christian unity. There is one "evangelization of America." To the Puritans of
the Massachusetts Bay Colony and the Franciscans planting the mission churches along the California coast, the one evangelization
"appeared as a single reality." In view of the mutual execrations hurled
at that time between "Protestant heretics" and "superstitious papists,"
it may seem doubtful that Catholics and Protestants viewed their evangelizing efforts as "a single reality."

Yet, forced to the wall, Puritan and papist knew they had more in
common with one another than with Iroquois or Aztec. Whatever their
disagreements—disagreements made more intense by their similari-
ties—both thought they were bringing the light of the gospel to a world
in darkness. In the song of Zechariah, both worshiped the God incar-
nate who came "to give light to those who sit in darkness and in the
shadow of death, to guide our feet into the way of peace" (Luke 2). One
might think the pope is putting a check on the ecumenical spirit, however, by referring to "the only Church of our Lord Jesus," meaning the
Roman Catholic Church, but then he adds "of which they are an
organic part." The "they" in question is all those, Protestant and
Catholic alike, who contributed to making America "mostly Christian."

Juan Diego Meets Cotton Mather

These subtleties play an important part throughout the synod. Arch-
bishop Francis George of Chicago (soon to be Francis Cardinal
George) speaks in the general session on the ways in which North
America is incorrigibly Protestant, forcing immigrants from Latin
America to adjust to a Catholicism that depends less on culture than

on individual intention. And, of course, to speak of other Christians as an "organic part" of the one Church bears on the synod's reflection about the "sects" and the ways in which all Christians are truly but imperfectly in communion with the Catholic Church, as the Second Vatican Council teaches. Amidst the subtleties of the opening homily is the allusion to "safeguarding the originality" of each way of becoming Christian and being Christian. And that brings us back to Our Lady of Guadalupe. Whether the newly discovered unity of America, which is the constant refrain of this synod, really amounts to much may depend in significant part on whether Americans—North, Central, and South—find in her story the "originality" of a Catholic way of being American and an American way of being Catholic.

The first apparitions are reported to have happened between December 9 and 12 in the year 1531, in a poor district on the edge of Mexico City called Tepeyac. There Our Lady appeared first to Juan Diego, and then to his uncle Juan Bernardino, whom she healed. In his synod intervention, a Mexican bishop will object to the common practice of calling Juan Diego a "peasant." That, we are told, is a European term, while Juan Diego is the representative of a new thing, the American. In any event, Mary finally appeared in the form of a miraculous painting on the cloak of Juan Diego, the very painting and the very cloak that are today on display in the Basilica of Our Lady of Guadalupe, where millions of the faithful go on pilgrimage every year and where miracles beyond numbering have been reported over the centuries. Of course there are skeptics, but both the cloth and the painting have been subjected to the most scrupulous scientific examination, and there seems to be no reasonable doubt that the first is authentic and the second inexplicable. Some Catholics in North America—perhaps because, as Archbishop George suggests, they are more Protestant than they know—are embarrassed by this sort of Marian piety. For a good many Latin American bishops, however, the pervasively popular and intense devotion to Mary and miracle is the Catholic trump card in the contest with "the sects."

The Iberians had definitively crushed the Aztecs in 1521, and with that the world of the indigenous peoples appeared to be irretrievably lost. A very good thing, some might say, since Aztec civilization was based on, inter alia, the ritual slaughter of thousands of human beings in order to appease its gods. But an argument can be made that almost any identity is better than none. The loss of identity and, along with it, a sense of personal and communal dignity, was a catastrophe. All that was changed by the surprising events at Tepeyac in 1531. There appeared a new being, the Mestizo, at the same time both European and Indian and yet neither. Speaking in Nahuatl, Our Lady told Juan Diego about the One who had ended human sacrifice by sacrificing himself on the cross. In the painting, her dress is European but the decorations are indigenous, and her face is Mestizo. She is certainly not a native goddess, but neither is she simply the Madonna of so many European representations. This is something new. To use the term now so current, this is the deepest "inculturation" of the Christian story.

Over her womb is the Nahuatl symbol for the new center of the universe, who is Christ. The Semitic Mary, the European Madonna, and the Aztec maiden all come together in Our Lady of Guadalupe. She tells Juan Diego, "Do not be afraid, you have nothing to fear. Am I not here, your compassionate mother?" It is hardly the case, as some contemporary scholars would have it, that Guadalupe first manifested the feminine aspect of God that had been lacking in Christianity until that time. What happened at Tepeyac can only be understood in the context of centuries of Catholic devotion centered in the Marian *fiat*—"Let it be to me according to your word"—in response to the angel's announcement that she was to be the Mother of God.

But at Tepeyac the feminine tone of radical responsiveness, of self-abandonment, and of maternal compassion was indelibly printed on the Catholic character in America. The contrast with the Puritan Bay Colony's obedience to the immutable decrees of a sovereignty that transcends all human knowing and feeling is striking. They are not different religions, to be sure, but they are very different Christian sensibilities. Weaving their way through the many subjects addressed by the Synod for America is always this question of what it means to be a Catholic American and an American Catholic. In a "mostly Christian" America, this synod reflects a conflict on its way to becoming a dialogue, perhaps, between the Puritan Cotton Mather and the Mestizo Juan Diego, under the patronage of Our Lady of Guadalupe.

I have to confess, however, that putting it that way may give the impression that this synod is more coherent, and less of an argumentative muddle, than in fact it is. The farther we get into this strange process, however, the suspicion grows that muddle and coherence may not be incompatible.

2

School Is in Session

How the Synod Works, and a Party with the Holy Father

IT SEEMS OBVIOUS from the interventions that some bishops would like to see changes in the structure of the synod itself. At the 1994 synod on the "consecrated life" of men and women religious, the last session witnessed a call to hold a synod on synods. That was understood to be a not very indirect challenge to the way Cardinal Schotte has been running the synods the last ten years and more. As the running of this synod made clear, the challenge, although backed by influential cardinals in the Curia and elsewhere, had little effect. It would seem that Cardinal Schotte's way has the support of the pope, who knows the tedium as well as, probably better than, anyone else. He has participated in every synod except one since they started after the Second Vatican Council.

The question of structure also arises in the form of suggestions that this unprecedented meeting of American bishops, North and South, should be institutionalized so that the new relationships established will not evaporate when the synod adjourns and everyone goes back home. At a deeper level that touches on the doctrine of the Church and its governance, as mentioned earlier, this synod, like other synods, is a continuing exploration into what the Second Vatican Council meant by "collegiality." When Paul VI established the Synod of Bishops toward the end of the council, in a document known as *Apostolica Sollicitudo*, he made clear that its purpose was to follow through on the council's decree, "The Bishops' Pastoral Office in the Church," and those who are generally viewed as progressives have long contended that the follow-through is far from adequate.

17

As we have seen, the pope is the president of the synod. With the assistance of the synod's general secretariat and a council of bishops, he determines the topic, sets the agenda, and finally decides the outcome of the synod's deliberations. This Synod for America—like the one on Africa before it and the other regional synods scheduled before the year 2000—is different in that anything and everything having to do with the Church in America is on the table. In the other synods that met every few years since 1965, a specific subject matter was named and then bishops from all over the world gathered to deliberate the subject posed. Thus, this Synod for America is narrower in its representation but broader in its focus. Some think it a strength and others a weakness that there sometimes appears to be no focus at all.

The Mission of Peter among Us

That, at the edge of the third Christian millennium, the Church in the person of Peter should address the state of the particular churches in different parts of the world seems eminently desirable. Were the pope to issue such messages without having very publicly consulted the leadership of those churches, he would certainly have been criticized for being "out of touch" with their particular circumstances. This despite his more than eighty pastoral visits to almost every part of the world, and despite the unprecedented attention he gives bishops during their *ad limina* visits to Rome. Minimally, then, the month-long consultation that is the Synod for America is necessary to enhance the credibility and effectiveness of the "exhortation" to America that he is expected to offer within the next year.

But the synod is much more than that. What John Henry Cardinal Newman in the last century called "the development of doctrine" is very much at work also with respect to the Church's governance. From the words of Jesus at Caesarea Philippi, "You are Peter, and on this rock I will build my Church," to Michelangelo's monumental basilica, to the interminable speeches in the synodical aula, Catholics believe that the office of Peter's successor is, despite everything, inseparable from the living voice of Christ. "To live is to change," Newman observed, "and to be perfect is to have changed often." At first appearance, the continuity of the papacy is much more evident than the change, but the change is undeniable, and with this pontificate quite striking. It is not simply that, just since Paul VI, the pope no longer wears the tiara representing a claim to temporal power, nor is he carried high above the heads of the faithful on a golden throne, nor does he take his meals in regal solitude, although those changes are not unimportant.

More substantive than this pope's having gone on skiing trips with friends, or regularly inviting scientists and philosophers for weeks of freewheeling intellectual exchange, or moving through countless crowds shaking hands and kissing babies, or singing along with Bob Dylan at a gathering of youth in Bologna a few months ago—more substantive than all that are his explicit and public reflections on what it means for the pope to be Peter among us. There is, for instance, the 1995 encyclical *Ut Unum Sint* ("That They May All Be One"), in which John Paul II invites other Christians, and especially the Eastern Orthodox, to collaborate in rethinking the exercise of the papal office or, as it is called, the Petrine Ministry. As the millennium now coming to an end has been the millennium of Christian divisions, he suggests, so must the next millennium be the millennium of Christian unity. Toward that end, he proposes that maybe the papal office should be refashioned along the lines of its exercise in the first millennium. It is conventionally said that the Church thinks in terms of centuries. This pope thinks in terms of millennia.

For Orthodox and Protestants, the great question is papal jurisdiction. They bridle at what they view as the monarchical and even dictatorial role of the papacy through much of this second millennium. Catholic teaching is that the papacy has "immediate and ordinary jurisdiction" over the universal Church of Christ. This pope has made it clear that unity is more important than jurisdiction, although the two are not entirely separable. Unity is also essential to the very mission of the Petrine office. Thus *Ut Unum Sint*: "It is obvious that the lack of unity among Christians contradicts the truth which Christians have the mission to spread and, consequently, it gravely damages their witness." While papal infallibility is much controverted among non-Catholics, and Catholic theologians explore the precise meaning of that dogmatic definition of the First Vatican Council, all agree that it is in service to the great truth of the indefectibility of the Church. Indefectibility means that we have Christ's sure promise of the Holy Spirit so that the Church will never desert or betray the saving gospel. But unity too is undeniably part of Christ's will for his Church. Again *Ut*

Unum Sint: "However true it is that the Church, by the prompting of the Holy Spirit and with the promise of indefectibility, has preached and still preaches the Gospel to all nations, it is also true that she must face the difficulties which derive from the lack of unity."

With a very personal and almost yearning desire for a new day, John Paul II speaks in this encyclical and elsewhere of the scandal that the Petrine Ministry, which Christ instituted to serve the unity of Christians, has all too often been an obstacle to unity. "I am convinced," he writes in *Ut Unum Sint*, "that I have a particular responsibility in this regard, above all in acknowledging the ecumenical aspirations of the majority of the Christian communities and in heeding the request made of me to find a way of exercising the primacy which, while in no way renouncing what is essential to its mission, is nonetheless open to a new situation."

Also at this Synod for America there are complaints that other Christians, especially the Orthodox, have not responded in kind to John Paul's bold initiatives for unity. Some Orthodox and Protestant leaders have said that the qualifying phrase in the above passage—"while in no way renouncing what is essential to its mission"—means that Rome is not prepared to change at all. But that is to miss the entire point. The point is an unprecedented invitation to others to join in a rethinking of the Petrine Ministry, including a rethinking of "what is essential to its mission." No pope in the last thousand years has spoken in this way, but however bold John Paul's initiatives, they are clearly intended to strengthen, not weaken, the Petrine Ministry.

The idea that the governance of the Church should be "democratized" in a way that would effectively dismantle the authority of the papacy is no part of his vision. The strengthening of the office that he seeks is not a matter of increasing the jurisdictional power of the papacy. Rather, it means enhancing the purpose of the Petrine Ministry, which is to strengthen all the members of the Body of Christ, and most particularly the bishops, who are the Church's apostolic leadership through time. Around the dome of St. Peter's basilica, in letters six feet high, are the words of Jesus from Matthew 16:18–19: *Tu es Petrus, et super hanc petram aedificabo ecclesiam mean et tibi dabo claves regni coelorum* ("You are Peter, and upon this rock I will build my Church and I will give to you the keys of the kingdom of heaven"). Also inscribed is another word of Jesus to Peter: "I have prayed for you that your faith may not fail; and when you have turned again, strengthen

your brethren" (Luke 22:32). John Paul has alluded to that second saying again and again with specific reference to Christian unity. In view
of the fragmented state of the Christian movement and the prospect of
the "new evangelization" of the world at the beginning of the third millennium, one might think that all Christians would welcome this understanding of a papacy more effectively in the service of a common
mission. But things are not always as one might think.

The Synod of Bishops and the many particular synods held since
it was established are an experiment in collegiality internal to the
Catholic Church, but they are also a groping toward a model of governance that might serve a more unified Christianity in the next millennium. There are many ways to track the chief concerns of this
pontificate. They are reflected in encyclicals such as *Laborem Exercens*
(1981) and *Sollicitudo Rei Socialis* (1988), which set forth Catholic social
teaching, and especially in *Centesimus Annus* (1991), a reflection on
what makes for a just and free society, written in the wake of the collapse of the Soviet empire, a development in which John Paul played a
crucial part (some would say *the* crucial part). In *Evangelium Vitae* John
Paul posited "the Gospel of Life" against what he called the culture of
death evident in abortion, euthanasia, and eugenics. That encyclical
prompted a friend, an official in the Southern Baptist Convention, to
say, "You guys sure got a pope who knows how to pope."

A Pontificate Determined to Teach

The pontificate's service to the entire Christian community and to
world culture was magnified by the encyclical *Veritatis Splendor*, in
which John Paul made the theological and philosophical case for the
existence of moral truth that both binds and frees human persons and
communities. If one considers the encyclicals alone—and, of course,
they are only part of the many teaching documents of the pontificate—
it is arguable that this is the most assertive teaching pontificate in the
two thousand years of the Church's history, which reinforces the expectation that future generations will refer to John Paul the Great in the
way that we have for centuries spoken of Leo the Great and Gregory the
Great. It is evident also in the many speeches at this Synod for America

that the teaching initiatives of this pontificate have only begun to be assimilated. I expect that will be the work of many years to come.

The driving concerns of this pontificate can also be tracked through the topics chosen for the assemblies of the Synod of Bishops. The 1980 assembly was devoted to the Christian family, a subject that John Paul has addressed with unwavering urgency. Penance and reconciliation was the topic posed to the 1983 synod. In a more recent document, *Tertio Millennio Adveniente* ("As the Third Millennium Nears"), John Paul has made some Catholics nervous by insisting that the Church too must confess the sins committed by her children through the centuries if she is to begin the new millennium as a more compelling sign of reconciliation to the world. The nervousness has two parts: first, that enemies of the Church might exploit the admission of faults; second, that some may think it is being said that the Church herself, as distinct from her members, has sinned. Catholic teaching is that the Church, as the immaculate Bride of Christ, is sinless, although she is composed of forgiven sinners. But John Paul obviously believes that the risks of misunderstanding must be taken if the record is to be cleared for the Great Jubilee of the year 2000.

The year 1985 witnessed what was called an Extraordinary Synod to mark the twentieth anniversary of the end of Vatican Council II, and to pull together the lessons to be learned from its implementation, and nonimplementation. That was my first experience of a synod, when I was still a Lutheran pastor and was covering it as a journalist. As I am learning here at the Synod for America, there is no comparison between watching a synod from the outside and being personally embroiled in the process. There is no doubt that the Extraordinary Synod of 1985 was very close to the heart of John Paul, who, despite some misperceptions to the contrary, is through and through "a man of the council." As a young bishop and then as archbishop of Krakow, Karol Wojtyla was intensely involved in the council's deliberations. In 1969 he published a book giving a complete overview of the council's teachings, *Sources of Renewal.* He worked assiduously to implement the council's directions in the Church in Poland, and undeniably views his entire pontificate as an unfolding of the renewal for which the council called. Perhaps the most lasting contribution of the 1985 synod was the launching of the work that produced the new *Catechism of the Catholic Church*, a project proposed at the synod by Bernard Cardinal Law of Boston.

The synods of 1987, 1990, and 1994 took up, respectively, the "three states" of the Christian life—the laity, the priesthood, and the "consecrated life." The last is now the preferred term for what Catholics have commonly called the religious life, meaning the wide variety of vocations to religious orders, communities, and congregations devoted to sundry ministries. Here at the Synod for America there is a great deal of discussion about the priesthood and the laity, but the complaint is heard that the consecrated life has been almost entirely ignored. That will be remedied, it is said, in the final "propositions" presented to the pope. I see that press reports are saying that the synod's emphasis on the laity is a reaction to a document released by eight dicasteries (curial offices) just a few days ago, "Instruction on Certain Questions Regarding the Collaboration of the Non-ordained Faithful in the Sacred Ministry of the Priest."

The instruction intends to correct certain abuses, especially in liturgical practices, that might confuse the distinct roles of clergy and laity. That's understandable enough, but the document, unfortunately, is somewhat clericalist in tone. The "nonordained faithful" is an unfortunate phrase. One might get the impression that the ordinary thing for the faithful is to be ordained. I am reminded of Cardinal Newman's response when he was asked what he thought about "the question of the laity." He said, "We would look pretty silly without them, wouldn't we?" Anyway, and contra the press reports, I have not seen evidence in the general sessions or group meetings that the discussion of the laity is in reaction to the curial instruction. It has much more to do with the fact that, especially in Latin America, there is an alarming shortage of priests, and lay people are taking up the slack in all kinds of ways. There are interventions urging greater flexibility in ordaining men to the priesthood, but nobody is questioning that priests are essential or that only men can be ordained. Although maybe the intervention by one Canadian bishop intended to raise the last question. I will come back to that.

Before leaving the matter of synods in general, a word on how the pope himself views this relatively new institution. On this, as on so much else, he has left a paper trail. While John Paul recognizes that national and regional conferences of bishops represent an important form of collegiality, he has been much more emphatic about the collegiality exercised in the Synod of Bishops. This is evident in the record of the 1969 synod, which got caught up in dealing with the crisis surrounding the 1968 encyclical *Humanae Vitae* on human sexuality.

There, nine years before he himself became pope, Wojtyla spoke of how the synod's exercise of collegiality must not be viewed simply in administrative, sociological, or political terms, but in light of communion with God that binds together the whole people of God in a supernatural unity. In no way, he said, does the council's teaching about collegiality diminish the leadership of the pope.

> Collegiality appears also as a strong confirmation of that supreme authority in the Church which belongs exclusively to the successor of St. Peter. Indeed, if the coresponsibility of all the bishops for the good of the whole Church is included in the concept of collegiality, greater importance is given to that unique responsibility which belongs exclusively to him and in which he cannot be replaced by anyone, even by the entire college [of bishops]. Similarly, it pertains to him alone to give practical execution to the collegial action of all the bishops, seeking in it ever more mature expressions of the communion both of the bishops and of the faithful. It is to him, in fact, that the Lord said, "Feed my lambs," and feeding means also seeking communion with all.

Far from pitting collegiality against papal leadership, the Synod of Bishops reinforces both. This was the point of an address on April 30, 1983, more than four years after Wojtyla had become pope: "The Synod itself exhibits the intimate connection between collegiality and primacy. The task of the successor of Peter is also a service to the collegiality of the bishops, and, conversely, the effective and affective collegiality of the bishops greatly assists the primatial Petrine Ministry."

Heavenly Flights, Daily Routines

"The intimate connection between collegiality and primacy." I came to Rome eager to see how such a thing works out in practice. But there are also many other things to do in Rome. My way into the synod was aesthetically eased by going out for dinner the night before it began with Mary Ann Glendon of Harvard Law School, who is appointed an auditor to the synod, and George Weigel, who is writing what I expect will be the definitive biography of John Paul II. After dinner we go around the corner to the Church of Sant'Ignazio for a concert on the final evening of an international Palestrina gathering that had brought together choirs from around the world. Tonight the finalists are performing — choirs from Lisbon, Poland, Moscow, and Portland, Oregon, and they are in exuberance and exactitude unsurpassably beautiful. Well, the heavenly choirs will undoubtedly surpass these.

The effect was considerably aided by the magnificent acoustics and architecture of Sant'Ignazio. Begun in 1626, the church is in the high baroque style of the Jesuit Counter-Reformation, a style to be savored in moderate portions. The churches of Rome are full of it, of course, and there are those who say baroque, even the later eighteenth-century rococo, is the most deeply "incarnational" of styles since, with its extravagant depiction of angels, cherubs, and saints, it "brings heaven to earth." Perhaps so, but I expect a steady diet of such artistic busyness would mean that we would have headaches in heaven, which seems counterintuitive. High baroque leaves no visual silences, no spaces for imagination; everything is, no matter how wondrously wrought, oppressively explicit. But *de gustibus*, as they say. We were there to listen, and Palestrina's "Ave Maria," Nestor's "Jesu dulcis memoria," and the final rendition by the combined choirs of Rachmaninoff's "Ave Maria" put me in a perfect frame of mind for a synod that would evince, in the words of Cardinal Wojtyla, "the communion with God that binds together the whole people of God in a supernatural unity."

To believe that that is what a synod is requires a very robust sense of incarnational possibility. There we sit, all 297 of us, of whom 233 are synod fathers with voting rights. Voting rights in the twenty-six general sessions means that you get one chance to vote, in the very last session, and then only to mark your book containing the final propositions with a *placet* or *non placet* (It pleases or it does not please). Never mind, it is an impressive assembly, made immeasurably more so by the presiding presence of the one who is, to employ some of his official titles, Bishop of Rome, Vicar of Jesus Christ, Successor of the Prince of the Apostles, Supreme Pontiff of the Universal Church, Patriarch of the West, Primate of Italy, and Servant of the Servants of God.

He carries such titles lightly. Not, to be sure, because he takes the office lightly but because he seems so completely at home with who he is. In his informal little book that became a best seller, *Crossing the Threshold of Hope*, he says,

> Expressions such as "Supreme Pontiff," "Your Holiness," and "Holy Father" are of little importance. What is important originates in the death and resurrection of Christ. . . . The Pope is called the "Vicar of Christ." This title should be considered within the entire context of the

Gospel. . . . Christ is personally present in his Church, and is likewise present in each Christian. . . . "Vicar of Christ" has less to do with dignity than with service. The Pope is not the only one who holds this title. With regard to the Church entrusted to him, each bishop is Vicarius Christi. Thus, if with this title one wants to refer to the dignity of the Bishop of Rome, one cannot consider it apart from the dignity of the entire college of bishops, with which it is tightly bound, as it is to the dignity of each bishop, each priest, and each of the baptized.

There he sits, the vicar of Christ among the vicars of Christ, hour after wearying hour, day after wearying day. Sometimes he nods, sometimes he is reading a book discreetly kept beneath his desk. As to what he is reading, wags who think the synod all too tightly orchestrated say it is the final document that will be issued at the end of the month's deliberations. Mostly, he rests his head on his fist gazing out at the assembly, or covers his face with his left hand and peeks through his fingers at the cardinals in their red and the bishops in their purple finery—each with the *zucchetto* (yarmulke), and the short cape called a *mozzetta*. An American bishop who is an expert on such things remarked that he spotted a couple of prelates with another cape, called a *mantelletta*, who were not entitled to wear it, and complained that the great cape, appropriately enough called the *cappa magna*, was nowhere on display. I suppose he knows what he is talking about.

There is also the *fascia*, which cretins call a cummerbund with a sash. A *motu proprio* by Urban VIII in 1624 ordered that all clergy should wear it, and students of such matters insist that, despite Paul VI's modification of the rule 326 years later, that order is still in effect (I am told that those who are inclined to be refractory in this matter should be referred to Secretariat of State Directive No. 135705 and *On the Reform of Choral Dress*, Sacred Congregation of the Clergy, October 30, 1970). As it happens, the *fascia* is today chiefly worn by higher clergy, and without the golden tassles on the sash affected by prelates of the Renaissance. The pope's *fascia* is white, of course, and made of watered silk; cardinals have red (scarlet, to be precise) also of watered silk, while patriarchs, primates, archbishops, bishops, apostolic protonotaries, and prelates of honor wear violet of ordinary silk. Although I am not disposed to argue the point, I am referred to a book on the subject that reads, "The practice since 1960 of draping the *fascia* bands one directly on top of the other, without the under section being entirely exposed, is contrary to historical practice." In the atrium outside the synod hall, prelates were regularly changing between street clothes and full dress. The place sometimes took on the appearance of a vast dressing room. It is, purists might lament, further evidence of the general decline of standards inaugurated by the deplorable 1960s that some of the bishops were indeed putting the bands right on top of one another.

So everybody—except those of us in the back rows in our plain black cassocks—is all dressed up, and this too underscores that what is happening here is not to be understood in terms merely administrative, political, or sociological. I ask myself if the "feel" of the event would be significantly different if everyone were in plain black suits and roman collar, or even suits and ties. For reasons I do not fully understand, I am sure the answer is yes. That would give it the appearance of a business meeting, and whatever else this synod is, it is not a business meeting in any ordinary sense of the term.

Not that Cardinal Schotte is not very businesslike. We have all received in advance the *Vademecum Synodi*, a handbook explaining what is going to happen, along with other documents, packed in a neat little briefcase made up just for the synod. At the beginning of each session, everybody is given an attendance card that is to be signed and handed in. This is true of the general sessions and of the small group meetings. These smaller circles are called *circuli minores*, but shortly people will be referring to them as the circus minores, from which ideas will go the circus maximus, where they will be disposed of by higher authority. I admit to being taken aback by a grade school regimen in which the putative princes of the Church—figures such as Cardinals Ratzinger, Arinze, O'Connor, and Laghi—are required to sign and hand in attendance slips. The *Vademecum* allows of no exceptions: "Those unable to attend the sessions are to give prior notice in writing to the President through the General Secretary, stating the reason for their absence." The rules say nothing about bringing a note from home. It is a little thing, but also a belittling thing, this business of the attendance cards. Perhaps it looms too large in my trying to figure out what is going on here. Or, just maybe, it is key to something important.

I have already mentioned the official languages: Spanish, English, Portuguese, and French, with Latin and Italian also permitted. Because of the way representation has been weighted, only about one speech out of eight is in English. The Brazilians, of course, speak Portuguese; the Haitians and some others from the Caribbean speak French, as do half the Canadians; and the general sessions are otherwise overwhelmingly in Spanish. In their interventions, a few bishops from the United States, including Roger Cardinal Mahony of Los Angeles, will demonstrate that they, too, speak Spanish. Thanks to several months with *Spanish in 10 Minutes a Day*, I listen simultaneously to the speakers and to the simultaneous translation, but mostly to the simultaneous translation.

Keeping Secrets

The *Vademecum* is very firm about "the obligation of secrecy." This gives me pause. "The texts of the Synod Fathers' interventions are documents destined for the Synod and therefore, once spoken in the synod hall, they become the property of the Synod and are not to be published." I am not clear on how this comports with the practice of a daily press briefing at which reporters are told what happened each day and are given summaries of the many interventions, or with bishops distributing their interventions and printing them in their diocesan papers back home, or with the publication of interventions in *Origins*, the publication of Catholic News Service in the United States. All of these things are routinely being done. Apparently this is necessary to make sure that secrets are accurately reported.

I am a neophyte when it comes to the mysterious ways of *Romanita*, but one might get the impression that secrecy here is mainly observed in the breech. A curial cardinal of long experience tells me that the difference between a secret and something really important is that the latter is covered by what is known as the "pontifical secret." A pontifical secret, he says, can take as much as several days to be leaked. That is probably somewhat jaded. I am reliably informed that some secrets have been kept for weeks. In any event, I take the secrecy rule imposed by the *Vademecum* as seriously as the next man. I am firmly resolved not to reveal any secrets that are still secret. Were that all resolutions were so easy to keep.

Words "Traveling by the Mouth"

The opening Mass is on Sunday, with the pope presiding and the synod fathers concelebrating. I will not attempt to describe the splendor of an all-stops-pulled papal Mass in St Peter's. What with jet lag and all, one bishop directly in front of me collapsed, quite overcome by it all. The ushers and medics rushed to his assistance with admirable alacrity, and the next day, quite fit again, he happily boasted of the distinction of having been treated by the pope's personal physician. It will make a great story back home. The doctor may be doing something good for the pope as well, for in the very long procession he walked unaided all the very long way down the nave of St. Peter's, to the delighted applause of the thousands in attendance. When, slowly and with obvious difficulty, he had walked around the back, climbed the steps, and emerged facing the people at the high altar, he raised his arms in the manner of a prize fighter acknowledging his victory. The people loved it, as did we all.

The next morning, Monday, the synod gets down to business, so to speak. The general secretary—that's Cardinal Schotte, of course—reads his report. It actually seems relatively brief, compared with what comes next. What comes next is the *Relatio ante disceptationem*, which means the proposal before the discussion. It is read aloud by the general rapporteur, His Eminence Juan Cardinal Sandoval Iniguez of Guadalajara, Mexico. As with Schotte's report, we have received this document well in advance. One assumes the moderately conscientious have already read it, but we follow along through the twenty-one closely printed pages as Cardinal Sandoval reads it word for word. It is essentially a reworking of the by now familiar *Instrumentum Laboris*, which is a reworking of the responses to the *Lineamenta*. The reworking of reworkings is a major part of the synod process. Much as with the cud of a cow, things are brought up again and again for rechewing.

The old adage that repetition is the mother of learning is taken very much to heart here. And the repetition must be oral. As an Italian monsignor explains to me, in Rome nothing has happened unless "it travels by the mouth." The several hours of being read to by Cardinals Schotte and Sandoval is good preparation for what is to come. Later in the synod we will read the lengthy *Relatio post disceptationem* (the proposal after the discussion), while Cardinal Sandoval "makes it happen" by reading it to us out loud. Finally, and most impressively, we will have still more hours of his reading to us the *propositiones* that are to be presented to the Holy Father, more than seventy of them, some of them being two or three closely printed pages, all in Latin.

Here again the carefully guarded secrecy of the proceedings intervenes. Secrecy apparently requires that the translator not be given the text in advance and, Latin not being his native tongue, he stumbles desperately, sometimes skipping whole sentences and even paragraphs. But the oral reading by Cardinal Sandoval is deliberate and punctilious, word for word. It must be an awful ordeal for him as well, but he puts on a brave face of very much enjoying it. Perhaps there is some rule that prevents him from alleviating the burden on his voice and our ears by letting one of the other synod secretaries help him out by reading portions of these excruciatingly lengthy documents. Sitting there right beside him, for instance, is Archbishop Francis George of Chicago, an accomplished Latinist who I am sure would be willing to help.

Of course this way of doing things gives the synod fathers plenty of time for prayer, meditation, and wool gathering at random. As my impatience mounts, I am making notes. I see here that I scribbled the first day, "Write a book!" It seems like a good way to redeem the time, and to sort out my thinking about this curious experience. Of course by this time the general discussion (*Disceptatio Generales*) has not even begun. The *Vademecum* advises:

> A generous block of time is given in the general congregations to allow for an exchange of information as well as to promote the expression of diverse opinions on the topic under discussion. . . . According to the dynamic established during previous general synodal assemblies, this period of time is dedicated to preparing something of a "mosaic'" through the active and patient cooperation of all the participants.

A "generous block of time" indeed, somewhat over seventy hours in all, minus the time we are being read to. The "topic under discussion" is elusive. For some reason, the reference to "preparing something of a 'mosaic'" puts me in mind of Mayor David Dinkins of New York, who was given to speaking of his notoriously inept administration as "a glorious mosaic." When you're not quite sure what you're doing, call it a mosaic, even "something of" a mosaic. But the *Vademecum* is undoubtedly right about "patient cooperation," meaning there's not much to be done about it. I make a note to reproach myself for being a curmudgeon. For the first of dozens of times, I remind myself that, if the pope is submitting himself to this, who am I to complain?

Doing Everything Dialogically

The *Vademecum* continues: "During this period, the Synod Fathers have the opportunity not only to listen to the group, but also to address the group, if they desire." Almost all desire. The day before you speak, you file a request to do so (called the *Postulatio Loquendi*), along with a summary of what you intend to say, which will be distributed to the press. The fathers get eight minutes to make their intervention. At the front of the aula are two large and two small television screens facing the assembly, and another on the desk facing the pope. These show who is speaking, with the name superimposed, but I note that most of the bishops crane their necks to get a look at the speaker in the flesh, which is a comforting sign that we have not surrendered completely to the virtual reality of the screen. Also at the front of the aula are two big electric boxes that flash three minute, two minute, and one minute warning signals to let you know that time is running out. Clergy, including bishops, are known to have weak terminal facilities. When time is up the microphone is shut off and, to the amusement of the assembly, many bishops rush desperately toward the end of their interventions when they see they are about to be silenced. One of the more senior cardinals of the Curia goes almost two minutes over his time and is not cut off. So status does have its privileges, even if he too must sign his attendance card and observe other aspects of the schoolboy regimen.

Cardinal Schotte is obviously not unaware of the discontent generated by the rules. His *Vademecum* observes, "It can be a little taxing to listen to so many interventions day after day, but in reality it is a very useful 'school' which fosters collaboration and collegiality." As he enters the aula at the start of general sessions and before he leads the assembly in prayer, the pope frequently has a little jocular greeting. This morning it was, "The teacher is here, now the class can begin." The image of the schoolroom is apt. The other day Cardinal Schotte greeted me at the entrance of the audience hall. "I suppose you are finding this somewhat boring?" Other synod fathers and I had discussed the procedure in a less than complimentary vein and maybe my remarks had been reported to him. "I must admit, Eminence, that parts of it are not scintillating," I responded. Apparently gratified that the plan was working so well, he smiled amiably and said, "Good. Good."

After 206 speeches in the general sessions, I lost count. Somebody says there were 267 in all, and that may well be right. Who knows? Well, Cardinal Schotte's office undoubtedly knows. I would say Who cares? but the answer to that is obvious. Most of those who spoke undoubtedly care a great deal about their own interventions. I know I certainly cared about mine. "The genius of this procedure," a veteran of past synods explained to me, "is that everybody gets to speak, and so everybody feels he owns part of the synod. He can look at the final propositions and see the part that he contributed." There is something to that, if you count the ands and thes in the final document. (Come to think of it, there is no "the" in Latin.) The synod secretariat is not bereft of a sense of humor. For instance, the *Vademecum* solemnly admonishes, "As established in the *Ordo Synodi*, the Synod Fathers are asked to *be very careful not to repeat subject matter treated amply by others*" (italics in original).

Then there are the small language-group meetings, fourteen meetings in all. Each has about twenty participants and here, of course, there is much more give-and-take. Unfortunately, meeting by language groups means that, with some exceptions, Latin Americans are talking with Latin Americans and North Americans with North Americans. This makes it difficult to engage the North–South differences that are so evident in the interventions in the general sessions. But our English group, and I expect the others as well, works hard at trying to keep that in mind. Press reports and a good many synod fathers observe that, in many ways, this is really a synod on Latin America. The intent is to prevent the really big countries from swamping the smaller ones. So, for example, the bishops conferences of the United States and Brazil get to elect one delegate for every twenty bishops in their conferences, while Ecuador, Bolivia, Nicaragua, and others get a delegate for every five bishops. In addition, the pope can make sure the synod is strategically imbalanced by appointing additional members on his own.

It is not only the North and South that are getting better acquainted. Latin America is very, very big, and many of the bishops there have little opportunity to know what is going on in other countries. From the North American College where I am staying, I ride back and forth with Anthony Cardinal Bevilaqua of Philadelphia. (Cardinals get a car and driver.) I've known him since his days as an auxiliary bishop in Brooklyn, and the other day he mentioned a conversation he had with a Latin American bishop during the coffee break. Whatever the subject was, the bishop said, "No, no, Your Eminence, you're thinking of Paraguay. The situation is very different in Uruguay. Paraguay is altogether another world." So it is not only the North–South divide that is being bridged here.

In the *circuli minores* phase of this process, our group elects Archbishop Rembert Weakland of Milwaukee as moderator and Bishop Donald Wuerl of Pittsburgh as reporter. Bishop Wuerl will have the opportunity to stay up all night for several nights conscientiously preparing a long report on our discussions, which will then go into the synodical mixmaster from which will eventually emerge the final *propositiones*. He says he counts it a privilege, and I do think he means it. In his role as moderator Archbishop Weakland, who is counted among the most "progressive" of American bishops, is generally genial, obviously wants to be perceived as fair, and is generous in sharing his observations on whatever is said by other members of the group.

In the small group, we talk about what we're going to talk about and vote on taking a vote, and it is all quite pleasant and parliamentary. The discussion is also substantive, as one would expect with participants such as William Cardinal Baum, Pio Cardinal Laghi, Archbishop Oscar Lipscomb of Mobile, Alabama, and the intellectually intense Archbishop Francis Stafford, formerly of Denver and now heading up the curial Office for the Laity. (Stafford was created cardinal shortly after the synod.) Sister Mary Waskowiak, who represents the Leadership Conference of Women Religious (LCWR), is here. In our first meeting, she urges that, whatever we do, it should be done "dialogically." That is unanimously approved. Also part of the group is Sister Mary Bernard Nettle, who is president of the Council of Major Superiors of Women Religious. That organization is much smaller than LCWR but is distinctive in that it is composed of communities that are actually attracting new vocations. Sister Mary Bernard does not speak much in the small group, but her powerful intervention in the general session about caring for the sick and elderly won warm and well-deserved applause.

Sisters Yesterday and Today

It is true that religious orders do not get much attention in either the general sessions or language groups. Brother John Johnston of the Christian

Brothers, who is an auditor, remarks that it is as though the last synod on the consecrated life had never happened. But there are many other and frequently more interesting discussions outside the formal meetings. For instance, a number of bishops have been reading the recently published book by Ann Carey, *Sisters in Crisis: The Tragic Unraveling of Women's Religious Communities* (Our Sunday Visitor Press). It is a carefully researched, understated, and utterly devastating account of the role of LCWR and others in getting women religious to follow the lead of progressive theologians in "renewing" themselves into virtual oblivion.

When the Second Vatican Council ended, there were almost two hundred thousand sisters in the United States who were working in schools, hospitals, nursing homes, and a wide range of social agencies —robust institutions built by impressive women who carefully guarded their authority against episcopal interference. Today there are less than half as many sisters, and their numbers are rapidly declining. Within the next two years, more than half of those remaining will be retired. Numerous institutions built by the heroic self-sacrifice of earlier sisters have now been handed over to secular control. That within such a short time so many communities moved from positions of vibrant leadership to geriatric dependence is a remarkable phenomenon. Among those associated with LCWR, many of the active remnant are among the most aggressively disaffected groups in the Church, and some publicly declare that the vocation of their community is to go out of business. The last sister who can manage to get her wheelchair over to the wall switch will triumphantly turn out the lights.

An archbishop tells me over lunch in a delightful little place he has found only a few blocks from St. Peter's that urgent thought must be given to what happens to the property of dying communities. Some of them have many millions of dollars in buildings, land, endowments, and other assets. Put them all together and billions of dollars may be at stake. When a community gets down to a handful of members, he asks, what is to prevent a small group of enterprising women who may be completely uninterested in the historic mission of the community from joining up and seizing the assets for their own purposes? An experienced canon lawyer, the archbishop has worked with the legal aspects of religious communities, and he thinks such scenarios are far from unlikely. In fact, he believes they are becoming, year by year, more pressingly probable.

The *Wall Street Journal* recently had a story on the Daughters of

Charity, who run hospitals all over the country and have built up a two-billion-dollar reserve, in part by selling off less profitable hospitals. The jaundiced view is that there is a better return from the market than from taking care of sick people. Asked about their still-growing portfolio worth two billion dollars, the sisters explain, "No margin, no mission." It's a catchy slogan, and theirs must certainly be a big mission. But the Daughters of Charity still have thousands of sisters, so is not in the category of orders that concern the archbishop.

I mention the case of a Unitarian-Universalist church in New York that had an extremely valuable piece of real estate on Central Park West. Some ten or fifteen years ago, when the congregation had dwindled to almost nothing, an enterprising group of toughs from Harlem showed up one Sunday, officially joined the church, and instantly gained majority control of its considerable assets. I believe a state court later found some way to undo their coup. The archbishop says that is a useful cautionary episode but opines that canon law is very specific about the "alienation" of church property. On the other hand, he worries, religious orders can be notoriously independent of church authority. "It isn't as though these sisters are Unitarians," he observes. "But then, some of them don't seem to be very Catholic either. And who knows what a tiny group of old people half-way into Alzheimer's could be persuaded to do." The question is left there, unresolved, but he's sure the Church should be thinking about it. Many of these more interesting discussions take place outside the formal structure of the synod.

The Long Road to Propositions, and a Party

Back at the synod itself, the small groups are to discuss for several days what has been said in the hundreds of speeches in the general session. What has been said is presumably reflected in a document called the *Relatio post disceptationem*, the proposal after the discussion. From this discussion of the discussion emerges another cluster of documents, the reports from all the small groups. The cud is ever more finely chewed. The next day, we go back into general session for several hours so that the rapporteurs of the small groups can read their reports to us.

The report of one Spanish group has passages bristling with resentment of North America. This surprises me a little, since I thought there had been real progress on that score during the days of the general sessions. It is not clear whether the resentment is over North American indifference to Latin America or North American exploitation of Latin America. Maybe both. A Colombian bishop with a fine wit explained to me the other day: "We can't make up our mind. On the one hand, we say that all the problems of Latin America are caused by massive American intervention. On the other, we say that the remedy for all the problems of Latin America is massive American intervention." The report of the French language group is a splendid flight of abstractions, delivered with fine rhetorical panache. It is a linguistic convolution worthy of a theophilosophical address at the Sorbonne. Nobody seemed to know quite what to make of it. Perhaps it was a bad English translation I was listening to, although afterwards a friend told me it was every bit as good in French. The prize for this session goes to the report presented by Archbishop William Levada of San Francisco; lucid, succinct, persuasive. One hopes a lot of that will eventually find its way into the final propositions.

But we aren't there yet. The next day we go back into the small group to write up some preliminary *propositiones*. We discuss what propositions are needed, and then members of the group are assigned the task of writing them up. I'm assigned two propositions, one on Christian unity and another on support for the pro-life cause. Between sessions, various appointments, and the delightfully interminable meals, I almost don't get them done. That evening is dinner with a couple of archbishops, a well-connected curial official, and an American writer friend. The intense conversation goes on until past midnight, and then, after futile efforts to find an open entrance, we have to wake a Swiss Guard to let our friends into the Vatican, where they are staying. We imagine the headlines the next day about American archbishops breaking into the Vatican. Back at the North American College, I'm up at four knocking out propositions before Mass at six-thirty. The propositions sail through the morning meeting of the small group, as do almost all of the propositions drafted.

Here I have a confession to make. I skip the afternoon session. It is a small ailment, an infected ingrown toenail, but the nursing sister at the North American is adamant that it must be seen to. So it is off to the hospital. This is my first encounter with Italian medicine, and it is as they say. It is conducted with a wonderfully insouciant air of improvisation. Much in the same way as the Italians drive. After cleaning out part of the infection, the doctor kindly offered to "cut off." I think he meant the toenail, but maybe he had the toe in mind. In any event, I politely decline his generous offer, making a note to have whatever needs doing done back in New York. The serious thing, though, is that I completely forget to submit a note to Cardinal Schotte asking permission to be excused from the afternoon session. He hasn't mentioned it, so I don't know whether my absence was reported. I must remember to check with Archbishop Weakland on that.

Now that the small groups have sent in their *propositiones*, the general rapporteur and the small group rapporteurs stay up most of the night putting them together into an "Integrated List." This is then rapidly printed (there's that almost miraculously efficient printing office again) and distributed to the synod fathers the next morning, who then go back for several more sessions in the small groups in order to prepare individual amendments (*modi*) to the propositions, which amendments are then approved or disapproved (ours are all approved) and become the *modi collectivi*. At that point, just as you might expect, the general rapporteur, the small group rapporteurs, the special secretaries of the synod, and unspecified "experts" go into a prolonged huddle out of which comes the long-desired object of this entire exercise, The Final List of Propositions.

The next morning, at the twenty-fifth gathering of the *congregatio generalis*, we have the final propositions, all nicely printed up in a booklet. There are seventy-six of them, and at the end of each is a place to mark *placet* or *non placet*—it pleases me or it does not please me. This is not a secret vote, for each synod father, after marking his pleasures or displeasures, signs his booklet. Then the roll of the entire synod is called, each indicates his presence by saying *Adsum* (I am here), and hands in his book. It is now well into the evening, and that's it. Our work is done.

The next morning, Friday, December 12, there is a final general congregation for sundry greetings and salutations. Cardinal Mahony, president-delegate of the day, graciously thanks the pope for bringing us together. Apparently it is mandatory that this speech include some complimentary words about the structure of the synod and how well it was run, but I don't think the cardinal's heart was in that part of his speech. Around ten o'clock we adjourn for the concluding Mass, entering St. Peter's from the back and vesting in the great hall behind the bronze doors. Mass is followed by *Convivium cum Sancto Patre*, roughly

translated as a party with the Holy Father. This fine lunch goes on for
a long time, which is just as well, since I have the pleasure of being
seated with Cardinal Ratzinger and my own bishop, Cardinal O'Connor, and the lively conversation touches on many points of interest.

Not to go uninterrupted, however. Cardinal Schotte is pleased to
announce to the convivium the outcome of the votes on the final
propositions. It is impossible to understate the level of suspense. But
he goes through the tally, one by one, all seventy-six of them. I am not
keeping score, but I notice that others are. I suppose they think that,
after a month's process of producing them, they should know the final
outcome. Suffice it that none of the propositions is approved unanimously, and none has more than trifling opposition. On many propositions there is only one *non placet*, and in my mind I imagine there is
one bishop in this crowd who is really unhappy with the entire proceedings of the past month and voted *non placet* every chance he got.
Since the booklets with the votes are signed, you can be sure that the
appropriate authorities know his name.

All in all, the *convivium* is most convivial, and it concludes with a
brief speech by the Holy Father and his apostolic blessing. He expresses
his great satisfaction with the synod and says it puts him in mind of his
days at the Second Vatican Council. Since he is almost the only one here
who was also there, he would know about that. I cannot help but think,
however, that the deliberations at the council must have been very different. At the same time, I am aware that in these last few days my view
of the synod has been changing. The suspicion grows that, through the
tedious repetition and seemingly wasted time, maybe more was happening than I thought at first. I will have to come back to that.

Meanwhile, these reflections attempt to convey something of how
one participant actually experienced the Synod for America. I have left
out one important piece of the proceedings. There is the *Nuntius,* or
"message," of the synod (not to be confused with the "exhortation"
that the pope will deliver in a year or so). The intended audience for
the "message" is the Church back in America, and it is an interesting
and frequently eloquent document. The consideration of the first draft
of the *Nuntius* provided the only opportunity in the general sessions
for an open exchange about a specific document and the specific questions it addressed. It was, as we shall see, a refreshing change.

But now it is time to turn to the substance of the questions
engaged by this Synod for America.

3

Why Are We Afraid?

The Many Americas of the "One America"

WE'RE COMING TO THE END of the second week, and at the beginning of a morning session Father Kolvenbach of the Jesuits hands me his signed attendance card to be passed on to the aisle where the attendants collect them. Most of the secretarial and logistical assistance here seems to be handled by the Legionaries of Christ. "You are ready for more of this unusual experience?" asks Father Kolvenbach. I suggest that the American phrase for it is cruel and unusual punishment. We are in the middle of the hundreds of speeches in general session, addressing what seems to be everything under the sun, or at least under the sun that shines on the Western Hemisphere.

I make a note that there is no way one could write about this seriatim without triggering in the reader a MEGO (my eyes glaze over) factor of irresistible proportions. The structure of the proceedings inevitably results in a hodgepodge of interventions, since nobody knows what is going to be said before or after he speaks. That is modified a little as the weeks go on. Those who wait long enough before asking to intervene can respond to what was said by others two or three days earlier, as Archbishop Levada of San Francisco very effectively does in challenging remarks by a Canadian bishop on the importance of dialogue with dissenting views. More on that below.

So I will try to impose a modicum of order on this account by arranging the story of interventions according to the subjects addressed. There is, for example, what might be called the "culture question" that is provoked by having a meeting on "America" in the singular. Ambivalence about what is meant by "America" is palpable

and driven by different, and sometimes contradictory, anxieties. With
the possible exception of that one bishop who seems to have voted *non
placet* on everything, it is unanimously agreed that it is a Good Thing
that bishops of North, Central, and South America are getting to know
one another better. How much farther that agreement can be pressed
is far from obvious. So what is the significance of "America" in the
singular?

Father Thomas Reese, S.J., is reporting on the synod for *America*
(in the singular), the Jesuit weekly, and he thinks the use of "America"
is nothing more than a typical instance of the Vatican following the
usage of old European geography books. Father Reese is the author of
a handbook on the inner workings of the Holy See, called *Inside the Vatican*. Returning from a session of the synod, I meet him outside the tall
iron gates beyond which the Swiss Guards admit only those with an
official pass. Garbed in blue jeans and 1960s journalistic casual, Father
Reese is hanging out with other American reporters who are no doubt
excellent sources. I am with a friend who cannot resist saying, "But,
Tom, I thought you were *inside* the Vatican."

Father Reese takes a deeply jaundiced view of this synod, compared
to which I am the very soul of credulous docility. In a report on the
synod he concludes: "Perhaps it is time to stop looking to bishops for
answers and solutions. Now it is time for economists and politicians, scientists and teachers, entrepreneurs and workers to make the New World
a more united and just community." My impression is that Father Reese
has not been looking to bishops for answers and solutions for a some
time. Be that as it may, I'm sure this is not called the Synod for America because the Vatican Library doesn't have an updated atlas. One reason I am sure is because many people, including the Holy Father, reflect
at length on the significance of "America" in the singular.

Living Together in "One America"

Early on, Archbishop Theodore McCarrick of Newark, New Jersey,
makes a big impression with a well-crafted speech on "this new world
of one America." He urges that the goal of the synod is that we should
all "understand, empathize, and become advocates of the third world."
He seems to be suggesting some kind of new episcopal structure to link

together the bishops' conferences of North and South, and his intervention clearly meets with evident approval, at least initially. Archbishop McCarrick has an international reputation as an effective fund-raiser. His presentation results in his receiving the overwhelming vote of Latin Americans to serve on the continuing council that will come back to Rome to rework the *propositiones* into their absolutely final, final shape for presentation to the pope, who will then rework them in preparing the final exhortation. I suppose that never in the history of a deliberative body have propositions been so thoroughly digested. This cow has seven stomachs.

A few days later, John Cardinal O'Connor of New York takes a somewhat different tack from that suggested by Archbishop McCarrick and others. He begins his intervention with a forceful appeal for a "new eucharistic crusade" as the key to the Church's renewal in America. Then, in his typically wry and self-deprecating manner, he allows as how he is "likely to lose what few friends I have left" by what he is going to say next. What he says next is that he thinks that any kind of new episcopal bureaucracy between North and South is a very bad idea. Cardinal O'Connor is known not to be a big fan of the national episcopal offices that are already in place, since they tend to discourage bishops from being bishops, turning them into branch managers who take their cues from national headquarters. In an assembly like this, it is easy to tell the superstars. The body language of deference and the clustering of conversation circles testify to O'Connor's status as a superstar. Everybody from "Alaska to Tierra del Fuego," as it is said here, knows who Cardinal O'Connor is. It's not only that he is archbishop of New York City, but he also serves on ten of the major dicasteries in the Curia. Most of the bishops here will, at some time or another, have business in Rome that will likely come before Cardinal O'Connor.

Of course it is the eloquence and logic of his intervention that carry the day. (I might say that even if he were not my bishop.) In a conversation of several years ago, he remarked that he gets up every morning with the prayer that he will get through the day without discouraging any impulse of the Holy Spirit. It is a rule that might be recommended to all bishops. I have often reflected on that, and it is closely related to what he is saying here. Of course there should be closer connections and greater cooperation between North and South, he says, but let it be "bishop to bishop, diocese to diocese, parish to parish." In other words, the Holy Spirit works through personal initiative and personal encounter, not by establishing some new secretariat that gives us the feeling that we have addressed a concern and can then go back to business as usual.

O'Connor, who speaks in English although he is quite fluent in Spanish, has the full attention of the assembly. He has over the years traveled extensively in Latin America and developed close relations with episcopal colleagues there. His is the last intervention before the coffee break, and when he finishes a Chilean bishop turns to me with a smile, "Well, I guess your cardinal just blew that idea out of the water." There will be no new North–South bureaucracy. The matter is not mentioned again, except obliquely by one bishop from Peru, who says that personal commitment is more important than new institutions. "Don't put the cart before the ox," he declares.

A Bitter History

The "new world of one America" theme plays out in subtle and various ways. On the Latin American side, I have already mentioned the ambiguity of North American interventions being viewed as both the problem and the remedy. A Colombian bishop explains to me that Latin Americans have good historical reasons for being uneasy about the "one America" idea. The First Pan-American Conference was convened in Washington in 1889, and the language of Pan-Americanism has long been associated with what is commonly called the gunboat diplomacy of the United States. Latin Americans well remember FDR's grandiose Pan-American visions, and JFK's "Alliance for Progress," most of which, despite Kennedy's personal popularity, they view as schemes to advance gringo imperialism. And they remember Nelson Rockefeller, who was FDR's "czar" for Latin America. I have several times been told about, although I have not seen, a 1944 Rockefeller report that called for the "Protestantizing" of Latin America in order to more easily incorporate it into the U.S. capitalist hegemony. There is a rumor that I have not been able to verify that the Vatican toyed with calling this a "Pan-American Synod." That obviously would not have gone down well with the Latin Americans.

"The new world of one America" sounds like motherhood and

apple pie, which is to say that it sounds very North American. There is an additional ambiguity cropping up here. The "one America" theme appears to run into conflict with the strong emphasis in speech after speech on the importance of indigenous cultures and national identities. Remember the bishop's assertion that Paraguay is an entirely different world from Uruguay. Moreover, there is a puzzlement over the frequently stated claim that "one America" reminds us of the "universality" of the Church. One North American asks me, "Are we really supposed to believe that as Catholics we are in closer communion with Latin America than with Africa, or Europe, or Asia?" She thinks that an odd view of the universality of the Church.

There is much talk about the "bonding" that is going on here, and it is no doubt a great thing for bishops from North and South to get to know one another and resolve to help one another. But, given the composition of the hierarchy in the United States, it seems doubtful that the universality of the Church will mean that most American bishops will feel a closer communion with Ecuador than with, for example, Ireland. Nor should it be forgotten that for many Latin Americans the ties to Spain and Portugal are at least as strong as those to North America, or to the other parts of Europe to which North Americans feel most attached. I am told, for instance, that more Latin American bishops have French as a second language than English.

For the North Americans, of course, an important factor is that Ecuador—and the Dominican Republic, Honduras, Nicaragua, and, above all, Mexico—are posing a very immediate challenge to the Church in the United States in terms of immigration. Because much of the immigration is undocumented ("illegal" is the impolite word) nobody knows the precise figures, but the best estimate is that Hispanics are now one quarter to one third of the total number of Catholics in the United States. As we Americans like to say, we are "a nation of immigrants," and some blithely assume that these new immigrants will be assimilated as were the millions of Irish, Italians, Slavs, and Germans who came before them. Unlike those earlier immigrations, however, the new immigrants are not bringing with them their own clergy, nor are they building the religious and cultural institutions to meet the needs of their communities.

Cardinal Bevilaqua makes a striking intervention on the dimensions of the challenge, asserting that by the year 2050 over sixty per-

cent of the population increase in the United States will be Hispanic.
Archbishop George of Chicago says that in contemporary America
immigrants have only one generation in which to be solidly claimed
by the Church; otherwise they will be lost to other religions or, more
likely, to a pervasively secular culture. Several Latin Americans have
mentioned in conversation that these discussions have been a real eye-
opener, or, as one put, a "true ear-opener." Clearly, some of the bishops from the South had not realized the dimensions of the Latin
immigration to the North nor the pastoral urgency that the bishops
in the United States are bringing to the challenge created by that
immigration.

Three weeks into the synod, one bishop said to me, "I thought we
were coming here to demand that you people take Latin America seriously. But now I see that you really do." He was perhaps being polite,
but there is no doubt a change in the atmosphere as the synod goes on.
A Mexican says with surprised delight, "I had no idea so many of your
bishops speak Spanish." It is a little thing, but then maybe not so little.
In the first week of the synod, I note that the Latin Americans, also
those who I know speak good English, insist upon speaking Spanish,
although they know my Spanish is pathetic. I take it to be a point of
pride, an assertion that this Synod for America is their synod too, and
maybe their synod mainly. In other words, "You must take us seriously."
By the third week this has changed. Those whose English is better than
my Spanish readily switch to English. I suppose that too is what is
meant by "bonding." It is a subtle but substantive evidence of trust that
they do not have to make the point about being taken seriously. And
that is surely no little thing.

I continue sorting through my notes on hundreds of interventions,
trying to group those that make significant contributions to what I am
here calling "the cultural factor." It is not an easy task. Perhaps one
intervention out of ten contains something substantively new. Given
the mind-numbing regimen of the synod process, that is inevitable.
One imagines how different it would be with a different approach in
which specific topics are proposed and then those who have something
to say about the topic at hand have the opportunity to say it. As it is,
everybody thinks he is supposed to make an intervention, and it can be
on anything that is somehow related to the Church in America, which
means it can be about almost anything. It sometimes seems to be very
close to talking for the sake of talking. After all, we have to fill up

twenty-six general sessions and nineteen small group meetings of several hours each. Minus, of course, the hours spent in being read to.

And yet, if one manages to stay awake, and if one listens attentively, and if one takes careful notes, and if one tries to sort out the substance from the rhetorical fluff, many very good things are being said here. An alternative is to do as the distinguished archbishop a few rows to my right. I have watched him now every day. As soon as the Holy Father has finished leading us in prayer, he sits down and promptly goes to sleep until it is time for the coffee break or closing prayers. Sometimes he snores, and the archbishop in the next seat gives him a collegial nudge. He nods his thanks and goes back to sleep. It is one way of getting through this endurance test, and he enhances the proceedings with one speech less.

A Minority of a Minority

There are a few interventions that change the synod, becoming points of reference for other interventions and for the innumerable discussions outside the aula. An outstanding instance is Archbishop George of Chicago on the religio-cultural differences between North and South America. During the course of his varied ministry, George has acquired an intimate knowledge of the several Americas and is impressed that, while they have all been shaped "in dialogue with Christian faith," in the North, with the exception of French Canada, it was Protestantism that did the shaping—not just Protestantism but, very significantly, Calvinist Protestantism. The Puritan God is preoccupied with law, individual rights, and contracts, Archbishop George says. It is "a faith which cannot sustain the ecclesial tissue of Catholicism." More than they commonly recognize, Catholics in the United States are "culturally Calvinist." In a Protestant culture, the Catholic Church is viewed "as a source of spiritual and psychological oppression," and many Catholics have internalized the Protestant critique of the Catholic Church "without recognizing its source."

Hispanics coming North experience culture shock as they find themselves a minority within a Church that is itself a minority. In the civic religion of the new country, George observes, history is viewed as the story of individual liberty rather than of human holiness. Among

the many new realities to which they must adapt, "they must also learn
how to be Catholic in another way, a more intentional and, if you will,
a more culturally Protestant way." Some Hispanics who are otherwise
successfully assimilated have not learned that, and may be lost to the
Church. "An integral part of the new evangelization must therefore be
a new apologetics, a loving and nondefensive but clear response to the
arguments against the Catholic faith raised by those who misrepresent
God's word by reading the Bible as a code, on one side, and by those
on the other who believe all religions, but especially Catholicism, are
an illusion which destroys both personal happiness and critical scientific intelligence."

George has played an important part in the initiative known as
"Evangelicals and Catholics Together," or "ECT" for short. Launched
in 1992 by Charles Colson of Prison Fellowship and myself, ECT has
joined evangelical Protestants and Catholics in advancing various cultural tasks in the U.S. and in intensive theological exchanges. Likely
Francis George also has that venture in mind when he adds that "a
clear account of our own faith does not preclude a strengthening of
ecumenical relations and excludes evangelizing against another faith
community." In the course of his talk he also attempts to clarify confusions about two terms in the synod's stated theme—communion and
solidarity. "Communion," he says, "is a supernatural gift that presupposes grace and union with the Holy Spirit," sustained by the sacramental life of the Church. Solidarity is a human virtue, "a firm and
persevering determination to commit oneself to the common good,
because we are all really responsible for all." The archbishop's clarify-
ing of concepts has the additional merit of drawing verbatim on mag-
isterial teaching—the Congregation for the Doctrine of the Faith's
"Certain Aspects of the Church as Communion," and the encyclical
Sollicitudo Rei Socialis. Despite that, however, other interventions continue to confound "communion" and "solidarity," sometimes using
them interchangeably.

Other speakers will pick up, however, on Francis George's understanding of "the preferential option for the poor," a phrase now
entrenched in the teaching of this pontificate. "Solidarity reaches
toward communion," he declares, "when the Church proclaims to all
that the greatest poverty is not to know Jesus Christ." But it is his distinction between Protestant and Catholic ways of being Christian, and

the challenge that poses for Hispanic immigrants, that will occasion most discussion. The assumption for most Latin Americans in their own countries is that *of course* they live in a Catholic culture; not just pervasively Catholic but constitutively Catholic. An atheist in Brazil is unmistakably a Catholic atheist. Catholicism is, as it were, absorbed through the pores of the skin. Coming to North America, they discover that to be Catholic is a decision and a continuing resolve, not entirely unlike what Protestants mean, and Catholics must come to mean, by *conversion*—as in the synod's official theme, "Encountering the living Jesus Christ: Conversion, Communion, and Solidarity."

Daring to Be Culturally Catholic

There is Protestantism and then there is Protestantism. Archbishop George underscores the Calvinism so important to the American founding, with its emphasis on divine decrees and contract (covenant may be the more accurate term). In small group discussion and elsewhere, Archbishop Francis Stafford develops the implications of the Protestantism issuing from the Emersonian, transcendental, and revivalist traditions. He is impressed by the argument of Harold Bloom's *American Religion* that American Protestants are really gnostics. The self is a spark of divinity that enters into union with God through a personally experienced knowledge of Jesus. "Americans believe in a resurrected Jesus but not an ascended Jesus," says Stafford. His point is that a resurrected Jesus is immediately known through a born-again gnosis, while the ascended Lord is mediated through the Church—through teaching, sacraments, and the saints past and present. How to maintain this Catholic sensibility in a Protestantized religious culture?

Although not responding directly to George or Stafford, since the structure makes direct responses next to impossible, Bernard Cardinal Law of Boston speaks to some of the same questions. With respect to the suggestion that "solidarity" means that we can or should remedy all the injustices of the world, Law urges that we get real. Getting real means that we face up to our living in a world that is alien, often hostile, and largely out of our control—which, he says, is not so bad. It invites us to embrace St. Paul's wisdom that "we are strong when we are weak." Instead of fretting about negotiating our relationship with the surrounding culture, we should have the courage to *be* the culture that is the Catholic Church. "Catholicism is our culture," I scribble in my notes, and am reminded of Stanley Hauerwas's maxim: "The Church doesn't have a social ethic. The Church *is* a social ethic." Between Cardinal Law and Stanley Hauerwas, a Methodist teaching at Duke University, there are many differences, but they agree on that.

William Cardinal Baum is a quiet and holy man. He was archbishop of Washington, D.C., before he came to Rome, first as prefect for Catholic education and then as major penitentiary. In that position he is the official of final appeal, under the pope, in cases of church discipline involving "the internal forum," or matters covered by the confessional seal. Cardinal Baum appears as fragile as a porcelain figurine and is generally recognized as one of the most influential people in the Curia. His intervention follows the themes addressed by those of George, Stafford, and Law. If we are convinced that we have been given the truth, he asks, why do we sound so defensive? Bishops must rediscover the apostolic nerve "to teach the doctrine of the faith and to confute heresy." He cites the debilitating ways in which biblical scholarship is today largely divorced from the faith of the Church; indeed it is often posited against the faith of the Church. Bishops are too often unnerved by those who claim to be their intellectual betters. This frail little man pauses, and then says with great urgency, "Do not be afraid of the theologians!"

If we are hesitant and stumbling and uncertain about the prospects of "the new evangelization," Cardinal Baum suggests, we have ourselves to blame and must repent. What bishops do they do in the light of eternity, which should be reason both for urgency and confidence. We are the people who pray, *Sancta Maria, Mater Dei, ora pro nobis peccatoribus nunc et in hora mortis nostrae*—Holy Mary, Mother of God, pray for us sinners now and in the hour of our death. There is nothing angry in his intervention. It is hard to imagine Cardinal Baum sounding really angry. The tone is intensely pleading and almost puzzled. Why are we afraid? I note that his is one of the few interventions that refer explicitly to the "last things"—death, judgment, heaven, and hell. With everyone here, I tell myself, that can be taken for granted. Maybe it doesn't need to be said explicitly. At the same time, would a complete outsider who is listening in to these discussions recognize that here is a group of men whose determinative conviction is that souls are at stake, and the consequences are eternal? One must hope so. They would have recognized it in Cardinal Baum's intervention.

As Baum seems slight and fragile, Alfonso Cardinal Lopez Trujillo is large, robust, and fills the space around him. He is president of the Pontifical Council for the Family, and he is all over the synod, as he is all over the world, actively promoting the many causes entailed by that portfolio. He has an eye problem and sometimes wears dark glasses, and then he looks for all the world like an episcopal Mafioso. Personal amiability is joined to toughness in this intellectually acute bishop, who served as general secretary and president of CELAM, the council of Latin American bishops' conferences, before coming to Rome. Then he was viewed as the scourge of liberation theology, serving as the enforcer of this pontificate's determination to liberate "the preferential option for the poor" from its Marxist captivity.

His intervention comes early in the general sessions and, more than any other, runs up the flag of the encyclical *Evangelium Vitae* ("The Gospel of Life") with its call to contend for the culture of life against the culture of death. Abortion is a "massacre of immense proportions." Latin American bishops are right, he says, to protest that their countries are oppressed by the rich nations to the North. But the nature of the oppression is not grasped by Marxist ideology, which is "a giant that has collapsed." The new oppression is a "contraceptive and abortive colonialism" that is worse than slavery. Slavery controls the lives of others, the new colonialism denies the right to life itself. As Gregory the Great challenged the Church and the world, so must we. I note that several other Latin American bishops refer to Gregory the Great, who died in 604, and wonder whether he has a particular prominence in Catholic thought there. I must ask somebody about that.

The vigorous intervention of Lopez Trujillo does not seem to have much repercussion, however. The themes of *Evangelium Vitae* do not come together in this synod as a powerfully unifying cause for the Church in America. I don't know why that is. Maybe, again, it is because it is taken for granted. Some things go without saying, or so it is said. But it is also true that things don't go unless they're said. In our small group, I am asked to write the proposition on *Evangelium Vitae* and the culture of life. And it does end up in the final *propositiones*, but

it looks very much like one more thing among seventy-six others. I
expect the pope will set that to rights in the final exhortation.

The Faith That Endures

Here is Jaime Lucas Cardinal Ortega, archbishop of Havana, Cuba.
When Fidel Castro seized power in 1959, the then archbishop of
Havana was old and senile, holed up in a foreign embassy; it is said that
he was quite unaware of what was happening. The priests and nuns
were overwhelmingly Spanish. Anticipating the slaughter of clergy on
the scale perpetrated by the Republican forces during the Spanish civil
war, many of them fled, and more than a hundred who stayed were
later expelled by Castro. The Church in Cuba was devastated. Almost
forty years later, the Church is embattled but clearly making a come-
back. Cardinal Ortega is young, energetic, and articulate. As a young
man he served a sentence in one of Fidel's labor camps. He is credited
with being key to what appears to be Fidel's new accommodation to the
Church in Cuba, and of course everybody is keenly aware of the pope's
forthcoming visit to that afflicted island. Ortega has the attention of
the assembly as he speaks of ideological delusions that would confine
Christianity to the private sphere. The gospel is inescapably public in
nature and, together with other Christians, Catholics in Cuba are prepared to make their contribution in the public square. The Church
cannot help but evangelize, Ortega declares, because she knows that
the gospel is the option for the poor and everyone else, for at the heart
of the gospel is the truth that "the Incarnation is God's preferential
option for humanity."

Also from Cuba is Bishop Alfredo Petit Vergel, auxiliary of
Havana. His face is deeply lined, and one suspects he is a man who has
suffered much. He speaks movingly of what it means to be part of the
universal Church. Through the dark years of oppression, "We were
always able to tell ourselves, 'We are not alone.'" "We are weak now. We
have only 250 priests, but we know now that there will be many more.
We thank our fellow bishops; we thank the entire Church, for not for-
getting us." There are four Cuban bishops here and they communicate
a sense of hopefulness that the worst is past, that the Church has once

again demonstrated its sheer power of endurance. Human rights groups say that there are a thousand to two thousand political prisoners in Cuba, including many imprisoned for their public testimony to the faith. Nonetheless, in a matter of weeks the pope is coming, and the expectation is in the air that things will never again be the same.

The enduring power of Catholicism in the piety of ordinary people is a theme underscored also by Bishop Alfonso Cabezas Aristizabal of Colombia. He detects a note of unwarranted fearfulness in many of the interventions. "Why are we afraid for the future?" he asks. The "sects" exploit our lack of confidence, when in fact the Holy Spirit is active in innumerable small groups. His is among many references to small groups, or "base communities" as they were called in the days of liberation theology. But the references appear now to be stripped of any ideological attachment to Marxist class struggle. The bishop speaks of small groups of Bible study, prayer, and evangelization, of charismatic communities, and communities gathered around healings and apparitions. Such popular piety should not be despised, he says, because it is the strength of a "Catholic theology of creation that has everything to do with water, salt, light, and the experience of ordinary people." His is among the more memorable interventions.

The question of Catholic culture and popular piety is addressed also by Aloisio Cardinal Lorscheider of Brazil, who notes that among his people Good Friday is ever so much more important than Easter. Piety is centered in the Sacred Heart, the suffering of Christ on the cross, and the sorrows of his mother. Seven million people a year, he says, make pilgrimages to the Marian shrines. All this is to be respected, but a new evangelization requires a "new emphasis on the Easter victory and Christ as the way to the Father." A new catechesis must stress that "Jesus is the absolute revelation of the human, God's revelation of man to man." (The last is a favorite phrase of John Paul II.)

The cardinal doesn't mention the influences of Protestantism and the North, but he is perhaps suggesting that South America could do with some of the religio-cultural elements that, in their exaggerated form, are deplored by Archbishops George and Stafford. A strong dose of Easter hope and an intensely personal relationship with God through Christ, can turn people to thinking of themselves as active subjects, rather than passive objects, of historical change. To be sure, the choice should not be between the suffering God of Catholicism and the sovereign God of Calvinism. I am perhaps going beyond what Lorscheider intended to say, but the juxtaposition with other statements on the cultural differences between North and South is suggestive.

Sorting Out Minorities

The first general applause for an intervention greets Bernardin Cardinal Gantin's description of the part played by African-Americans in the religious history of the continent. Gantin, a most imposing exemplar of black manhood, is prefect of the Congregation for Bishops, and he traces the role of black leaders through the history of Brazil, Haiti, Panama, Colombia, and the United States. Martin Luther King, Jr., gets mentioned, although I don't think His Eminence is suggesting that he was a Catholic. When it comes time for propositions in the small groups, an American bishop says, "We simply have to make a strong statement about African-Americans. It is expected of us." That is not uniformly welcomed by Latin Americans, however. Many of the bishops here are "people of color," but they make clear that they do not think of themselves as African-Americans. That is a North American term, they say. In the South there is also African blood, but the racial and ethnic mix is much more complicated. One South American bishop even protests the regular reference to "Hispanics." "We are not Spanish. Most of us are indigenous peoples who, under the influence of Spaniards, adopted the Latin Rite."

A North American view of racial realities is poignantly reflected in the intervention of Mrs. Jacqueline Wilson of the Office of Black Catholics in Washington, D.C. Politely but pointedly, she complains that the synod's preoccupation with Hispanics is shortchanging the importance of blacks in the United States It is a delicate point. There are about one million African-Americans among the sixty million Catholics in the United States. It seems evident that Catholics do not view black Americans as a major "mission field." In part because most priests and bishops think less in terms of mission fields than in terms of serving populations that are already Catholic. In part, too, because evangelizing blacks, who are overwhelmingly Protestant, might be seen as distinctly unecumenical. But in largest part because the pastoral challenge of twenty million or more Hispanics in North America simply overshadows any sense of urgency about reaching African-Americans.

The tendency to focus exclusively on Hispanics is pointedly questioned also by Bishop John Cummins of Oakland, California. What about Asian immigrants? he asks. He notes that the *Instrumentum Laboris* twice says that immigration to America is "basically from Europe and to a lesser extent from Asia." Far from being "lesser," Cummins notes that in the last decade seven hundred thousand immigrants came to the United States from Europe and more than two million came from Asia. There are 7.2 million Asians in the United States. "To put the church's pastoral challenge in perspective," he says, "let it be noted that the Asian population in the United States today is equal to the population of Bolivia and greater than the populations of Paraguay or Uruguay. The number of Asians in the Archdiocese of Los Angeles alone is greater than the entire population of Guyana or Suriname."

Against America's sometime hostility to Asian immigrants, Bishop Cummins cites the *Catechism of the Catholic Church* to the effect that "the ultimate end of the whole divine economy is the entry of God's creatures into the perfect unity of the Blessed Trinity." That might strike some as an unlikely premise on which to base U.S. immigration policy, but the bishop is on solid ground when he notes that Asian immigrants are receptive to Catholicism, and Chinese Catholics in particular might someday have a place in the Church in the United States comparable to the role they play in Singapore, Indonesia, and Malaysia. He cites the observation of two bishops in Asia that "the new Mediterranean Sea, *mare nostrum*, is the Pacific Ocean." I sense there is some ambivalence about Bishop Cummins's argument. He is further complicating the picture. As though the wide variety of questions entailed in something called a Synod for America is not already maddening enough. There are no interventions directly taking up Cummins's point, but it has made its mark. A Brazilian says on the way out: "Sometimes I think you Americans are saying that you have other concerns than Latin America. You have, how do you say, other fish to be cooking." He too has a point.

Evangelization as Oppression

The subject of indigenous peoples figures prominently in our discussions, although it is not always clear what people we are talking about.

Of North American bishops, two claim some measure of Indian blood, Archbishop Charles Chaput of Denver and Bishop Donald Pelotte of Gallup, New Mexico. (The latter explained to me how his city got its colorful name, but I forget now.) When the subject of indigenous peoples comes up in our small group, a very progressive nun reproaches Archbishop Chaput for speaking of "Indians." They now want to be called Native Americans, he was informed. No, he responded, that was a couple of years ago. "Now the preferred term is Indian again." It's not easy to keep up with the nomenclature of racial and ethnic deference. In his major intervention, Chaput does not talk about indigenous peoples, but the bishop of Gallup does.

We should thank God, he says, that so many indigenous people have been baptized, "but vast numbers were robbed of their cultural identity. Many indigenous people remain ambivalent about Christianity, and many others reject it completely. . . . As pastors, we must make it clear that we are sorry for past mistakes and actively seek reconciliation." Here we are back again to the question of the "first evangelization" and the "new evangelization," contemplating the wounds of "1492 and all that." Listening to some of these interventions, I cannot help but think of Francis Parkman's incomparable history, *The French and English in North America*, recently republished by the Library of America. His graphic telling of the missionary heroism of the Jesuits and the brutality—dare one say savagery?—of the Iroquois is profoundly incorrect in today's climate.

One wonders what the North American martyrs, whose shrine in the Albany, New York, diocese is so sorely neglected today, would think of our apologies for their sacrifice. To be "robbed of cultural identity" is no doubt a bad thing. But cultural identities can be riddled with moral ambiguities, and it would be helpful to have clearer distinctions between, for instance, robbing people of their identity and bringing them the gift of the gospel. What is it that St. Paul says? "From now on, therefore, we regard no one from a human point of view. . . . If anyone is in Christ, he is a new creation; the old has passed away, behold, the new has come. All this is from God, who through Christ reconciled us to himself and gave us the ministry of reconciliation" (2 Corinthians 5:16).

Of course there is the matter of the "inculturation" of the gospel, based on the Catholic principle that grace does not destroy nature but brings it to perfection. The tensions in the relationship between the "old" of culture and the "new" of Christ are very subtly treated in the 1991 encyclical, *Redemptoris Missio* ("The Mission of the Redeemer"). Maybe I missed a mention of it, but it seems to be among the many major teaching documents of this pontificate not cited in these hundreds of interventions. The assembly is obviously taken with the talk of Harry Lafond, a chief of the Crees in Saskatchewan and appointed an observer to the synod by the pope. Addressing the pope, he says, "Grandfather, we greet you, the Crees of my community and all of us First Nations peoples of Canada." Chief Lafond says we must talk and listen to one another with compassion, and "must protect our Mother Earth, who is constantly under attack by large corporations interested only in profit. . . . We must become risk takers and dialogue on subjects leading to tremendous changes." Among the changes he proposes is the ordination of Indian elders and the inculturation of rites and ceremonies. Those recommendations are seconded in two later interventions.

At the later *convivium* with the Holy Father, Chief Lafond makes a dramatic appearance in a large and splendidly feathered headdress, and blue jeans. An Italian cardinal asks me *sotto voce* and without evident irony, "The blue jean. Is that authentic Indian garment?" I allow that I do not think so. Later, the cardinal abandons Roman indirection. "Is it really so important, all this talk about indigenous cultures? Is it not what you Americans call political correctness?" He is right in part, of course, but, as Bishop Pelotte noted in his intervention, inculturation is also a subject frequently addressed by the pope. But how to acknowledge that "mistakes" were made by the first evangelizers without implying that it was a "mistake" to evangelize? The Oblates of Mary Immaculate (OMI), who played such a large role in the evangelization and education of Indians in Canada, have made statements that come very close to apologizing for the gospel of Christ—and not in the sense of Francis George's call for a new apologetics. (Archbishop George is himself an OMI.)

Latin Americans may be right in thinking they have handled questions of race and indigenous identities better than we in the North, although the color-calibrated stratification of societies from Brazil to Puerto Rico give reason to doubt it. Indian policy in the North has swung wildly—from extermination to smothering paternalism, with

both Indians and non-Indians deeply divided about what now is the
course of justice. It does not reflect in any way on the sincerity of the
bishop of Gallup and others, but there is a touch of irony when those
who are the eminently successful products of thorough cultural assim-
ilation are the champions of maintaining a distinct cultural identity
that they have themselves left behind. But, as it is said, history has
many ironies in the fire.

The Canadians

These are especially thorny problems for the Canadians. Perhaps more
than anywhere else, the Church in Canada has in recent years been
plagued with an epidemic of scandals related to sexual abuse, not least
in church schools for Indian children. The ten Canadian bishops here
are a conspicuous presence. They have their own problems of cultural
identity, obviously wanting to distinguish themselves from the bishops
of the American giant to their South. In addition, the French-speaking
Canadians have yet other distinctions to maintain, from the English-
speaking Canadians and also from other French-speakers such as the
Haitians. Bishop James Wingle of Yarmouth, Nova Scotia, thinks I go
too far in saying that the subject of Canadian identity is Canada's major
intellectual industry, and he may be right. But he agrees that it is a very
big cottage industry, and understandably so. Bishop Wingle and I were
born in the same town in northern Ontario and have much to discuss
during the course of the synod.

I suppose there are several ways the Canadians could distinguish
themselves here. They could, for instance, identify themselves with
some of the more radical-sounding Latin American critiques of the
American imperial hegemony. They are distinguishing themselves in
two other ways, however. First, they seem to be the only national group
that is getting together every night to coordinate their interventions
and collectively approve of their texts. The general rule is that a synod
father should indicate whether he is speaking in his own name or on
behalf of his national conference. The great majority of interventions
are individual. The Canadians speak collectively. Several synod fathers
observed that the Canadian interventions had the flavor of being written by a committee, with the texts distributed willy-nilly for individual

bishops to read in the aula. They have hit upon a second, and somewhat curious, way of distinguishing themselves from the Americans,
namely, by sounding hyper-American.

Several of the Canadian interventions are as close as the synod
comes to what might be called the *National Catholic Reporter* wing of
the Church in the United States. This is reflective of the disposition
that Archbishop George no doubt has in mind when he speaks of those
who have been, often unknowingly, Protestantized in their understanding of Catholicism. Bishop Gerald Wiesner of British Columbia,
for example, speaks for the Canadian conference on the question of
women in the Church. He refers to the many areas in which women are
the "primary participants" in church work, thus implicitly touching on
what is often viewed, also in the United States, as the problem of the
feminization of religion. But his concern is not that. His concern is
about exclusion, specifically the reservation of the priesthood to men.
In Canadian culture, he notes, "any form of exclusion is seen as discrimination" and there is "a common view that all matters are open to
discussion." Therefore, "the issue of women and ordination is deeply
divisive within the Canadian Church."

It is a carefully crafted statement, walking up to an assertion that
the magisterium is wrong in saying that it is an infallible teaching that
the Church has no authority to ordain women, but stopping just short
of saying that. One can, with some effort, resist the inference that the
Canadian bishops believe women's ordination should be an open question. The difficulties of those who disagree with church teaching are
very sympathetically depicted by Wiesner. "In our day, women have
become deeply conscious of their dignity and rights. At the heart of
this consciousness is a radical transformation of self-awareness and
self-understanding." "Privately and in solidarity with others, women
have been exploring the question of what it means to be female at this
time in history. The outcomes of this search, both positive and negative, are still unfolding, but what is abundantly clear is a heightened
sensitivity to all signs of discrimination, marginalization, and exclusion." And so forth.

What is also abundantly clear is that the cultural circumstance he
describes has produced a transformation, maybe a radical transformation, in the Canadian bishops' understanding of what it means to
represent the Church's teaching. What Bishop Wiesner sees as sympathetically dialogical others view as defensively reactive. "In Canada," he

says, "the use of inclusive language when addressing persons of both sexes has become standard to the extent that deviations from this norm are conspicuous and, for some, offensive." The garbled syntax is, for some, puzzling, if not offensive. One might think that persons who are of both sexes would be a very small minority indeed. And since, in both English and French, people are addressed in a second person singular or plural that is not gender-specific, one very much doubts that a deviation from that norm has become standard in Canada or anywhere else. The linguistic confusion about the niceties of language notwithstanding, it is evident what the bishop is getting at. He is greatly impressed by a small minority of women who adamantly refuse to recognize that a term such as "mankind" is gender-inclusive.

But Bishop Wiesner has certainly raised eyebrows here with the suggestion that women's ordination is, or should be, an open question. In informal discussions, opinion is divided as to what the Canadians are up to. I hear one or two bishops say the Canadians are courageous for raising forbidden questions, but most seem to be shaking their heads in bemusement. Yesterday Bishop Raymond Lahey of Newfoundland made his intervention. He is in a particularly awkward position, since the Church in Newfoundland has in recent years been shaken to its foundations by the exposure of widespread patterns of sexual abuse that had been going on for years. "In the Americas today," he says, "the Church is less rejected than marginalized."

Speaking in the name of the conference, Lahey urges that the way to respond to this circumstance is to follow the example of St. Paul at the Areopagus in Athens. We must take the risk of dialogue. "Sometimes dialogue demands critique. To proclaim the gospel is to preach the cross of Christ. In purely human terms, this will always be scandal and folly. But any critique will be accepted only when the gospel has been heard, and hearing depends upon the church using the categories of the culture." Bishop Lahey is impressed that "at the Areopagus, Paul, whose only boast was the cross of Christ, did not preach the cross." This seems a bit strange. According to Acts 17, it was because Paul told them about the death and resurrection of Jesus that "some mocked, while others said, 'We will hear you another day.'" Among Paul's missionary initiatives, the Aeropagus was not a conspicuous success.

It is true, as Bishop Lahey notes, that John Paul II has spoken of a "modern Areopagus" and urges that the gospel be proclaimed in a manner that is intelligible to those who hear it. With the Holy Father, however, there is no doubt that it is the gospel that is to be proclaimed. Lahey says: "Faced with marginalization, the Church too often attempts to preserve the gospel rather than communicate it. Frequently, it simply repeats religious language the culture finds meaningless, thus further marginalizing itself." St. Paul, says Lahey, "brought the gospel into the culture in a new way that risked a former language and understanding." But wasn't the reaction of mockery and dismissal precisely because his gospel challenged the regnant cultural assumptions of Athens? It was their former language and understanding, not Paul's, that was at risk.

There is no denying that the Canadians are raising interesting questions. Bishop Lahey favors communicating the gospel rather than preserving it, although one wonders how it can be communicated if it is not preserved. Perhaps the confusion is with what is meant by the gospel. "The gospel is 'the news of great joy for all the people,'" he says. "This truth, and the positive values people live out in very diverse situations, creates the potential for a 'dialogue of salvation' with all of sincere will." The gospel truth, it seems, is what people accept as joyful news and is in accord with the positive values of people of sincere will, no matter what it is that they sincerely will. That at least is as close as Bishop Lahey, speaking for the Canadian bishops, gets to defining the gospel that is to be communicated rather than preserved.

More precisely, it appears the gospel is to be defined by the positive values and diverse life situations of the very people for whom the Church has been marginalized. By such a missionary strategy, so to speak, we are given to understand that the "dialogue of salvation" may save the Church in Canada from its unhappy marginalization. Must not the Church, Bishop Lahey asks, reach out to dialogue with "women . . . gay and lesbian persons . . . those concerned about environment and population . . . those in the New Age movement" and, not least of all, "with those who are 'pro-choice' and others who struggle with the Church's teaching on personal morality, on the basis of the Church's doctrine that morality is a matter of free, informed choice, in conscience, providing such choice is not destructive."

From all these parties, presumably, the Church has much to learn. Such dialogue is not without its perils, the bishop allows. "For the Church," he says, "it involves risk: the risk of being unfaithful or being misunderstood. Given the growing marginalization of the Church, however, there is far greater risk in no dialogue." After this intervention, I assure a synod father that I do not think the Canadian bishops meant to say that marginalization is a greater danger than unfaithfulness, although there is certainly a risk of that misunderstanding.

The Canadian fear of being rejected or marginalized, as St. Paul was rejected and marginalized at the Areopagus, appears to be premised on the view that Canadian culture is, as Bishop Wiesner asserts, "profoundly secular." One might ask, Compared to what? It is true that, according to the pertinent survey research, religious belief and behavior in Canada are not as high as in the United States. But it is much higher than in Western Europe and many other nominally Christian societies. Moreover, it is a timorous Church that trims its sails to the finding of survey research. Vatican Council II's references to "reading the signs of the times" was not a counsel of timidity. Canada, more than the United States about which he was writing, exemplifies the argument of John Murray Cuddihy's classic sociological study *No Offense: Civil Religion and Protestant Taste*. The hyper-Americanism of Canada's elite culture—a culture to which the Canadian bishops are finely attuned—is closely linked to the famous niceness of Canadians. One must, above all, give no offense.

Quebec after the Revolution

There is in Canada almost no awareness of what Americans mean by the "culture wars," no sense that in important ways the Church is and must always be countercultural. In Canada there is little that is comparable to the American phenomenon of "Evangelicals and Catholics Together," in which Catholics and evangelical Protestants understand themselves to be called to a common cause in restoring moral deliberation to the public square, and are not intimidated when the prestige media (and much of the liberal religious media) disparage them as "Christian conservatives" or even "the religious right." The posture of many Catholics in Canada—standing hat in hand and asking to be accepted, or at least not despised, by the elite culture—is also tied to a uniquely Canadian factor that can be summarized in one word: Quebec.

The history of French Canada is often depicted in terms of Catholic oppression comparable to the worst stereotypes of Franco Spain or "priest-ridden" Ireland. In retrospect, everyone agrees that the earlier concubinage between Church and government in Quebec was unhealthy. Whether it was the stifling, life-denying, ghettoizing oppression that it is now commonly said to have been is another matter. In the 1960s, young turks such as Pierre Elliott Trudeau, the former Canadian prime minister, powerfully assisted by priests and bishops caught up in the excitements of Vatican II, successfully launched what they frankly called a revolution to liberate Quebec from its Catholic captivity. With stunning rapidity, paralleled only by the Netherlands, Quebec went from being one of the most religiously observant societies to one of the least observant. Schools, hospitals, and social services were rigorously secularized; priestly vocations evaporated; Mass attendance plummeted; the churches were emptied; and politicians and priests together declared the revolution a success.

Not all the priests, however. I talk with them when I serve some small churches in Quebec, where my family has a summer cottage and I try to spend a few weeks each year. A now elderly priest from Montreal, who was back then a champion of the revolution, has second thoughts. "In the old days," he says, "the Church had everything. We *were* everything in Quebec. Nobody even thought of questioning the priest, never mind the Catholic Church. It was an unnatural situation. We should not go back to it even if we could." Then he adds, "But we did not realize how much would be destroyed, or how quickly. We wanted to liberate them from the repression of the Church and we ended up liberating them from the Church."

The result, he says, is that even younger priests today, of whom there are a few, are afraid to say or do anything definite lest they be accused of wanting to return to the bad old days. He is not prepared to say that the remedy of the revolution has turned out to be worse than the disease it aimed to cure, but he agrees with other clerics in Quebec in saying, "Ours must be the quiet generation." Maybe the time for proclamation will come again, it is said, but this is the time for dialogue. The question of how many silent generations the Church can survive goes unanswered. Nerve once traumatically lost is not easily recovered. It probably requires something like conversion—as in "Encounter with the Living Jesus Christ: The Way to Conversion, Communion, and Solidarity in America."

Dialogues Timorous

While the structure of the synod militates against direct responses to what has been said earlier, there is no doubt that Archbishop William Levada of San Francisco is responding to the Canadians. Not to the Canadians alone, but to the Canadians in particular. He does so politely. "In mentioning these questions," he says, "I count on the trust which undergirds our affective collegiality and which is so evident at this synod." That is put very nicely. On how the Church should bear its public witness, he quotes the catechism: "From this loving knowledge of Christ springs the desire to proclaim him, to evangelize, and to lead others to the yes of faith in Jesus Christ." The confident witness of bishops will inspire confidence in the laity, he says, citing the words of John Henry Newman on the laity: "I want a laity who know what they hold and what they do not, who know their Creed so well that they can give an account of it and who know enough of history to defend it. I want an intelligent, well-instructed laity. . . . And one immediate effect of your being able to do all this will be your gaining that proper confidence in self that is so necessary for you."

A gospel that is carefully preserved and confidently communicated, suggests Levada, could lead to something like renewal. "What a great service—a true *diakonia*—we bishops, who are the principal teachers in the Church, together with our priests and catechists, would give to our people by making them confident evangelizers of their culture—empowering them to speak to their contemporaries about the vocation of marriage and work, about the dignity of life and human sexuality, to strategize in government and boardroom and marketplace about the obligations of justice and our mutual responsibility to provide for the poor as our brothers and sisters in the one family of God."

Of course the Church's message must be inculturated, he notes. "Like you, perhaps, I grapple with what this means. Since cultures are by definition different expressions of our common humanity, an inculturated catechesis will involve different approaches, histories, and themes." What it does not involve is any suggestion that the Church's message is uncertain or up for grabs. "All the more important, then," says Levada, "that we bishops recall our primary duty as members of the apostolic college to preserve the unity of faith in our pastoral action." Bishops, he proposes, might take their cue from the pope, who

certainly listens, but listens in order more effectively to speak the gospel, and who is certainly not marginalized, as "we have seen for ourselves in papal visits to our cities and countries, at events like World Youth Day, and in the call to a 'new evangelization' in preparation for the third millennium."

Dialogue is undoubtedly important, but authentic dialogue is in the service of truth. In response to questions that have been raised in this aula, Archbishop Levada says he has some questions of his own. "Might not a call for 'dialogue' with women about their concerns, without explicitly saying that according to our faith holy orders can be received only by men, run the risk of creating ambiguity or be mistaken for lack of clarity or certitude, thus undermining a genuine evangelization?" He has another question: "If we 'dialogue' about discrimination toward homosexuals, do we not also have to 'evangelize' them about the true meaning of human love and sexuality written in nature and revealed in Christ?" On this question Levada speaks with some personal authority. "My own experience in San Francisco has shown me how easily dialogue can be overtaken by political pressure. The city's human rights commission named me as contributing to a 'climate' of discrimination against homosexuals because I said public recognition should not be given to so-called gay marriages."

No "Catholic Moments"

There are no formal responses to these and other questions posed by Levada, but conversations over coffee and lunch indicate a general recognition that a marker has been laid down. Notably about the bishops' "primary duty as members of the apostolic college to preserve the unity of faith in our pastoral action." One reporter says the next day that Archbishop Levada made a conservative speech demanding that bishops toe the party line. At least for that reporter, Levada had given offense. In the aula I think the Archbishop is understood to be saying that dialogue is not a synonym for vacillation or faintness of heart. At least I hope that is what he is understood to be saying, since I am sure that is what he intended to say.

In this way, through the course of hundreds of speeches, the "cul-

tural factor" is addressed. Archbishop McCarrick's "new world of one America" contains many cultural worlds. They are the worlds of the one world called America, which hardly exhausts the universality of the Church, yet contains most of the pieces representing the whole. The Protestant (mainly) North and the Catholic (mainly) South, both endangered by what Stafford calls gnosticism and, closely related to that, both oppressed by what Lopez Trujillo's calls the imperialism of the culture of death. Both susceptible to an immanentism that militates against Cardinal Baum's concern for "the last things." Both in need of Cuba's testimony to suffering fidelity, and the confidence articulated by Cabezas Aristizabal that God is God of everything, and therefore we dare not be afraid. Both North and South, and the worlds within each, are caught up in sorting out collective identities and what it means to inculturate the gospel. All are agreed on the importance of dialogue, provided it is a dialogue born of boldness and not of fear.

The "dialogue of salvation" is not a dialogue in search of the meaning of salvation but a dialogue that presupposes the meaning of salvation, says one bishop. Dialogue means that we do not have all the truth and have much to learn from others, says another. "It's another good word that's been spoiled. I don't use it anymore," a cardinal tells me. "It's a word liberals use when they are really saying, 'Let's keep talking until you give in and we win.'" Tensions within the Church and tensions with the surrounding culture reveal strikingly different dispositions, ranging from timorousness to belligerence, with numerous variations on both. The differences sometimes follow conventional lines of liberal versus conservative, but only sometimes.

Almost nobody from the North has a kind word to say about the culture in which the Church finds itself. Secularization, materialism, the hostility of the mass media, pornography, the decadence of popular entertainment—all are repeatedly, and no doubt deservedly, deplored. The Church is depicted as being on the cultural defensive, with some urging a strategy of appeasement and others a strategy of confrontation. I have not one note of an affirmative word being said about the cultural context that has permitted Catholicism to flourish in North America as it has in few other parts of the world. Certainly no sustained argument has been made that the Church can or should seize the initiative in transforming the culture. That sense of a moment of opportunity—what the New Testament calls a *kairos*–is not conspicuous in these proceedings. A

decade ago, I published a much-discussed book, *The Catholic Moment*, that made an argument along those lines. Its evident lack of influence, to judge by what is being said here, is humbling.

In fact, however, many of the North American bishops are not so defensive or so filled with a sense of being besieged as they sound. The North Americans are greatly outnumbered here, and they know they are viewed as the privileged minority in the one America. Any accent on positive aspects of the Church in the United States might seem jarring and runs the risk of increasing Latin American resentment of their privileged brothers and sisters to the North. There are exquisitely delicate sensibilities in play here. Better for the North Americans to say, in effect, "Yes, life is tough all over. We have big problems, too. Let us tell you about them." The synod tends to get bogged down in a one-upsmanship of lamentation. But it is fair to say that the Latin Americans come here with the bigger problems, ranging from massive poverty to political violence and instability to an acute shortage of priests to no money for much of anything. One advantage they do have—if the statements here are an indicator—is that they are on friendly terms with their culture. Theirs is, all in all, a Catholic culture. Worries are expressed about whether it will continue to be that, and most of those worries are centered on the cultural, economic, political, and religious impact of what is perceived to be *el coloso del Norte*—the colossus of the North. About that, as we shall see, the bishops have many, and frequently conflicting, things to say.

4

Slaying Economic Dragons

Desperation, Attendance, and a More Excellent Way

A S THE OLDEST, LARGEST, and most representative institution in the world, the Catholic Church has no alternative to being inclusive, and it is so in ways that far exceed the imagination of today's champions of inclusiveness. James Joyce did not intend to be entirely complimentary, but he was surely accurate in describing the Catholic Church as Here Comes Everybody.

The papacy is key to the Church's universality. From the very beginnings of the Christian movement two thousand years ago, being in communion with "the successor to Peter" was an indispensable mark of orthodoxy. In the first millennium that communion was a theological postulate but in everyday reality something quite distant from the life of most local churches. By the twelfth century that had dramatically changed, and a monarchical papacy could convoke meetings of bishops from all over the Christian world, as in the ecumenical councils. The significance of this is described by Eamon Duffy in his *Saints and Sinners: A History of the Popes*:

> Councils also served to consolidate a sense of episcopal identity and collegiality, and thereby to evolve a potential counterweight to the emerging papal monarchy—as the popes would one day discover to their cost. They helped also to educate bishops into a sense of the Church as an international and not merely a regional entity. At the Third Lateran Council [1179], the prince-bishops of Germany and France rubbed shoulders with an Irish bishop whose sole income (as he explained) was derived from the milk from three cows, and the Pope consecrated two

Scottish bishops, one of whom had walked to the Council with a single companion. Such encounters played an important role in the medieval reimagining of the Church not as a communion of local churches, but as a single international organization, with the Pope as its head.

Although it is not a council, much the same can be said of John Paul II's presidency of this Synod for America, who sits where Alexander III sat more than eight hundred years ago at the Third Lateran Council and, *mutatis mutandis*, where all two hundred and sixty-one other successors of Peter have presided. (Depending on which historical authorities one consults, John Paul II is either the two hundred and sixty-second or two hundred and sixty-fourth pope.) Unlike the Scotsman, none of these bishops walked from America, and I doubt that any is solely dependent on three cows, but there is no doubt that many are poor, and their people even poorer. Also as in the twelfth century, a synod such as this teaches and reinforces the lessons of identity and collegiality. The tensions between the local churches and the universal Church are still very much in play, as they almost certainly will be until the end of time. Many things have changed, including the construction of national episcopal conferences since Vatican II, a development about which many in the Roman Curia are ambivalent. In the United States in the nineteenth century, Rome frequently saw itself as the champion of priests and people against imperious bishops, whereas now many think Rome must champion bishops against the imperiousness of episcopal conferences, constantly reminding all and sundry that in Catholic ecclesiology "the local church" means the diocese and not the national church.

The economic and political disparities among those whom the pope has brought together are stark. In the view from Latin America and the Caribbean, the United States and Canada are immensely, even scandalously, rich. The Archdiocese of New York alone, a Colombian bishop tells me, has a budget larger than the national budget of his country. Without knowing the exact figures, I don't argue the point. But he allows that the comparison does lose some of its force when one considers the hundreds of parishes, schools, and social services, plus dozens of hospitals, operated by the Archdiocese. Nonetheless, there is no disputing that the Church in America is, by comparison, very rich indeed.

Beyond Generosity?

Part of the complaint here, seldom stated in so many words but unmistakably clear, is that the Church in the North is not as generous as it ought to be. Several interventions, and also the final propositions, praise the churches in Europe, and especially in Germany, for their generosity to Latin America. North Americans refrain from mentioning in public, although it does not go unremarked in private, that the Church in Germany has lots of money to give away because its ordinary operating expenses are covered by government-collected taxes rather than voluntary contributions. Politely but firmly, Father James Ronan, an auditor who heads the Latin American desk at the U.S. bishops' conference, underscores in his intervention the extent of the help that flows from North to South. There are millions of dollars in aid through Catholic Relief Services, plus two thousand American priests and religious working in Latin America, a contribution of value beyond monetary calculation. In addition, three thousand U.S. parishes are "twinned" with parishes in Latin America, many of them providing generous financial help. Father Ronan is just a touch impatient, and justly so, with the invidious comparison between the United States and Germany.

Generosity, however, is not the crucial issue in the economic relationship between North and South. As is said in speech after speech, in tones sometimes plaintive and sometimes belligerent, the crucial issue is justice. Archbishop Weakland of Milwaukee is among the first to intervene as the general sessions get under way. He addresses the economic connections between North and South, and moves from there to the cultural. "Economic relationships," he says, "also affect, gradually but surely, the cultural values of the nations participating in such economic systems, because every economic system brings with it specific values and goals. We are becoming culturally, not just economically, interdependent." He refers to economic "globalization," a term that will recur thousands of times (or so it seems) during these weeks, and indicates that it poses a particular challenge to a Church that is also global. "How can we, as a Church that is universal and catholic, affect these interdependent economic trends and the culture that they are bringing with them?"

Right from the start, then, Weakland posits one way of conceiving the relationship between the economic and the cultural. Which has priority? Is cultural change driven by the economic system, or is culture, in the language of the social sciences, an independent variable? It is a question of many parts, and it has been disputed in many forms throughout the modern era. Marxist and related socialist theories have insisted on the priority of the economic. Economics is the phenomenon and culture the epiphenomenon. Catholic social teaching, and especially the teaching of this pontificate, emphasizes the priority of culture, which is finally the priority of the human spirit in relation to God. That argument is most impressively set out in the 1991 encyclical, *Centesimus Annus* ("The Hundredth Year"), which marks the centenary of Leo XIII's *Rerum Novarum*, which is generally taken to mark the beginning of modern Catholic social doctrine.

Weakland and others are by no means subscribing to an economic determinism in which culture, ideas, and the life of the spirit are epiphenomenal. In his intervention, Weakland speaks forcefully of the "values" that must temper and direct the economic. But on the relationship between the economic and cultural it is a matter of emphasis, and of underlying conceptualization. The economic-cultural connection is a theme that runs through the synod's many reflections on economic justice. It is seldom addressed explicitly but is unmistakably, if implicitly, evident in numerous interventions. One bishop complains that he detects in some interventions a desire to evade economic justice by "a retreat into the spiritual." What he sees as a retreat other bishops view as the Church locating its mission in the one sphere where it can make a real difference, namely, the cultural. By changing the culture—the ideas by which people understand themselves, their possibilities, and their responsibilities—other changes will follow, including the transformation of the economic sphere.

Forgive Us Our Debts

The repeated and vigorously pressed complaints of the Latin Americans are not usually framed in such theoretical terms. Bishop after bishop alludes to the "impossible burden" of the external debts owed by their countries. In the last two decades many countries borrowed enormous sums from institutions such as the World Bank and International Monetary Fund, as well as private banks—loans that they cannot now repay. In his reflection on the Great Jubilee of the Year 2000, *Tertio Millennio Adveniente*, John Paul II proposed a canceling, or at least a sharp reduction, of such international debt. From the *Instrumentum Laboris* through all the sessions, it is a proposal much discussed and about which there is much division. Toward the end of the synod, support for the idea seems to flag and it is missing from the first list of propositions to be presented to the pope, but then, inexplicably, it reappears in the final propositions.

"We must tell the truth," exclaims a Central American bishop in tones of moral indignation. "Those who loan the money are doing so to make money off these loans." No doubt. From this and other interventions, one might infer that the Church should return to its medieval condemnation of usury. The resentment over external debt, however, is not focused only on the United States and the international agencies that are largely controlled by the United States. Many bishops speak of how money borrowed by their countries is used to enrich politicians and their friends, never reaching the poor for whom the loans were supposedly intended. John Paul II has on several occasions also spoken with great candor about the problem of corruption in the political leadership of the debtor nations, and I suspect bishops are emboldened by his example. During the course of the synod, the press reports that several Latin American governments are publicly protesting what some bishops are saying about them here.

But the brute fact, it is repeatedly asserted, is that these nations simply cannot repay these debts. Archbishop Antonio Gonzalez Zumarraga of Ecuador says that every child born in his country already owes $1,200 to the external debt. An American remarks to me that every child born in the United States owes many times that amount to pay off our national debt, which may well be true, but $1,200 in Ecuador is a life's fortune. In his country, the Ecuadorian bishop says, thirty percent of the national budget is devoted to the external debt, and that is just to pay the interest on it. Bishops from other countries cite figures as high as fifty percent. It is true that the United States devotes more than twenty percent of its national budget to the same purpose, but it is pointed out that that is a very different matter for a

country with a flourishing economy. Many of the Latin Americans go on to detail how this money is stolen from what the government should be doing in education, medical care, and a host of other activities to help the poor. I am impressed that the mind-set reflected in many of these interventions is thoroughly statist. The assumption is that the meeting of an endless list of human needs is chiefly, maybe even exclusively, the business of the state. The rhetoric is reminiscent of Lyndon Johnson's "war on poverty" in its heyday, but, unlike the United States, none of these governments has trillions, or even millions, to spend on grand social experiments.

The recurrent complaint about economic injustice is directed at "neoliberalism." In most interventions by Latin Americans, the term seems to be a synonym for capitalism. Now that Marxist-oriented liberation theology is out of favor, it would not do to polemicize against "capitalist exploitation." The economic vocabulary of the South is much more shaped by European usage than by American, with the result that "liberal" and "conservative" have quite different meanings. In the United States, "liberal" connotes a collectivist and statist orientation, while in Europe and Latin America "liberal" refers to what in North America is commonly called libertarianism—a devotion to laissez faire capitalism. Neoliberalism is the capitalism associated with another buzz word of the synod, namely, "globalization."

The use of terminology is not always so clear, and there is considerable confusion about what this awful neoliberalism is supposed to be. One Spanish small group comes in with a proposition for the final list that condemns "neoliberalism" and all its works, and all its pomps, and all its empty promises. It sounds very much like the exorcism in the baptismal rite. The discussion in our circus minores comes to the conclusion that anything that does all the terrible things that neoliberalism is accused of doing should certainly be condemned, if only we knew what neoliberalism is. Some of us do suggest that neoliberalism is an alias for capitalism, but others say that could not be the case since, if the target is capitalism it might indicate that liberation theology is not as dead as we are assured it is. The resolution of these confusions that carries in the final *propositiones* is to refer to "so-called neoliberalism." Everyone can agree on condemning "so-called neoliberalism," since it leaves open the question of what the monster is, or if it is at all. The unanimous judgment is that the currently prevailing economic sys-

tem, whatever it may be called, is not meeting the economic needs of everybody in the Americas.

As neoliberalism is constantly linked to globalization, so it is also linked to "individualism." Individualism, in turn, is another word for selfishness. A Mexican bishop allows that neoliberal economics does not entirely exclude the poor, "but those who take advantage of economic opportunity do so for selfish reasons, only to help themselves and their families." One wonders if economic entrepreneurship that enables people to take care of themselves and their families is appropriately described as selfishness. If everybody in a nation did that, it might look very much like economic prosperity. I remind myself that it is too easy to criticize the economic bromides that these speeches provide in such abundance. The reality on the ground in many of these places is one of grinding poverty, combined with a sense of hopelessness, of being the impotent objects of economic decisions made far away in New York and Washington. And entrepreneurship, it cannot be denied, is connected with an individualism that may be seen as threatening to the communal bonds characteristic of Catholic cultures. The core perception that drives the economic complaint expressed here, however, is that "they" are so very rich and "we" are so very poor, "they" are getting richer and "we" are getting poorer, and such injustice must be condemned. Whether or not that perception is accurate, it is crucial to understanding what is being said here.

Bishop Alvaro Ramazzini Imeri of Guatemala intervenes colorfully on two subjects. The problem with our treatment of indigenous cultures, he says, is that "we are like the very compassionate fellow who took the fish out of the water so that they wouldn't drown." Then he urges that the economic and political problems of Latin America cannot be understood without addressing "the narco monster that has a thousand heads." Others will return to the question of drug trafficking, a business that dominates and corrupts some countries, especially in Central America. The several comments on this subject are balanced between criticizing regimes that collaborate in supplying narcotics and criticizing the North for providing the demand that makes the supply so profitable. It is an equation of supply and demand, and both sides of the equation are to be condemned. In the same intervention, one bishop indicates that the United States is guilty of not controlling its borders to stop the drug traffic and is also guilty of trying to control its borders to prevent illegal emigration from the South.

Bleak Realities

Much of what is said on these questions is impossibly wearisome in its repetitiveness, and heads begin to nod, also the heads of those who said much the same thing in their own interventions. "The rich get richer and the poor get poorer." "Radical and systemic change to make real the preferential option for the poor." "Place human limits on the market." "Demonic neoliberalism." "The idolatry of the dollar." "Economics that reduces man to a mere means." "Evangelize the economic order." "An economics based on the gospel of Jesus." "Put people before profits." And so it goes. The hackneyed phrases of more than a century's quarrel between controlled and free economics pile up one upon another in a ritualized reprise of all the clichés, catchwords, platitudes, and angry abstractions that have bedeviled the effort to think clearly about social justice. John XXIII's encyclical *Pacem in Terris* ("Peace on Earth") and Paul VI's *Populorum Progressio* ("The Progress of Peoples") are several times invoked. Those documents are often, and I think wrongly, interpreted as advocating a socialism-friendly pursuit of justice through the statist redistribution of wealth. John Paul II's *Centesimus Annus*, which accents the free economy's creation of wealth and the moral imperative of what it calls "expanding the circle of productivity and exchange," goes largely unmentioned.

One's impatience with the muddled and repetitious rhetoric is checked by several factors. Many of these bishops live in daily encounter with desperate and, or so it seems, unchangeable poverty. In the face of great evil, somebody must be held accountable, and it does seem that the United States is the best candidate for that. Some Latin Americans have an exaggerated notion of the political and economic influence of the bishops in the North, and they want them to use that clout to change the policies of America and the institutions of international finance. Moreover, few of the Latin Americans have any economic training beyond having picked up the catch phrases of liberation theology and, while eschewing the revolutionary aspects of that ideology, they still see economics through the prism of class struggle between the rich and the poor. By the end of the second week, however, there is a marked change in both tone and substance, demonstrating that, despite the laborious structure of the synod, there is something going on that approximates an exchange of ideas.

Bishop Vicente Cisneros Duran of Ecuador seems impatient with abstract attacks on an unjust world. "Evil is universal," he observes, with a touch of irritation that bishops should have to be reminded of that. People must take responsibility for their own lives, and for the state of their own societies. Alluding to pervasive political corruption that stifles economic improvement, he asserts, "We must have the courage to teach that there is an alternative, and that alternative is simple honesty." This and related themes are taken up by other bishops. Especially persuasive is Samuel Carter, a Jesuit and archbishop emeritus of Kingston, Jamaica. Here it is worth noting that the representatives from the Antilles (Jamaica, Guadeloupe, Santa Lucia, Trinidad) and from parts of the Caribbean tend to get slighted in these proceedings, so dominant is the Latin America presence.

Archbishop Carter is a large, avuncular man, and very Jamaican. In small group discussion he allows that he is no economist, "But I know that sensible people are not going to invest money where there is political instability and nobody knows what is going to happen tomorrow." Yes, he says, the external debt is a very big problem, but maybe it is more accurate to say that the money was stolen rather than borrowed, "And the people who stole it are our own leaders." He is sympathetic to the idea that debts should be canceled or reduced, but he is also worried about how that might be interpreted. "What are we saying here? The Church has always taught that if you borrow money you should pay it back. We should be very careful not to give the impression that we don't believe that any more. We're talking about big things like international organizations and globalization, but what message are we giving to ordinary people and how they should go about their daily business? If you don't pay your debts, people will stop doing business with you."

Several bishops, including Luis Morales Reyes of Mexico, counsel that there is a need for a new encyclical on ethics and economics. A couple of months ago Father Kolvenbach, the father general of the Jesuits, was reported to have said in an interview that work on such an encyclical is under way, which surprised a number of people in the Curia, and also, I expect, surprised the Holy Father. The pope is likely under the distinct impression that there already is an encyclical on ethics and economics, plus related questions pertinent to the just and free society. It is called *Centesimus Annus* and was published in 1991.

Sobering Specifics

Bishop Ivan Marin-Lopez of Colombia has a different idea. He submits that there is a need for an encyclical on charity. He challenges the proposition, widely promoted in recent decades, that concern for justice has made charity obsolete. The usual way of putting this is that charity deals with "Band-Aid solutions" while justice promotes "systemic change." Charity, however, is but a another name for love, and there is nothing greater than love. We need to cultivate, says Marin-Lopez, a "piety of the poor." It is too easy to call for grand transformations of the world order. We would be more believable, he urges, if we lived more closely with the poor, and then he gets disturbingly concrete by proposing that bishops agree to give up a significant part of their privileges and give away half their personal property in preparation for the Great Jubilee of the Year 2000. His intervention is not greeted with applause, but a good many heads seem to be nodding in agreement.

On questions such as international debt, some Latin Americans seem to believe that bishops in the North have only to use the considerable influence that is theirs. The report from one Spanish group declares, "The Church in the North will also have to appear as a mediator between governments and financial institutions and our people in the South on matters concerning foreign debt." Cardinal Law of Boston has already intervened to counter any delusions about the Church's clout in such matters. Cincinnati's Archbishop Daniel Pilarczyk, who is also former president of the U.S. bishops' conference, says he has learned a great deal here about the depth of Latin American concern about the external debt, but he very much hopes that what the synod proposes will "not sound hopelessly simplistic." He does not mention it, but in recent years the U.S. conference has issued a host of pronouncements on politics, economics, foreign affairs, and other matters that have raised reasonable questions about whether the bishops may be exceeding their competence. The credibility of this synod, Pilarczyk and others urge, will be enhanced if it does not claim to have answers it does not have, and if it does not promise solutions it cannot deliver. Nor will such claims and promises do anything to strengthen the collegiality between North and South that is being nurtured here.

Father Andrew Christiansen, S.J., works with the U.S. bishops' conference and is here as an auditor. He came equipped with some very specific information on the matter of international debt. Amidst the frequently soaring rhetoric of the synod proceedings, such specifics are in short supply. The current debt problem, he notes, goes back to 1973 when the OPEC countries quadrupled oil prices and then had to find places to invest their enormous profits. Commercial banks in the United States and elsewhere came up with the idea of making huge loans to poor countries just at the time that their economies were crippled by the high price of oil. In 1982, Mexico announced that it would not repay its debts and headed into an economic tailspin. Seeing that they were not going to get the money back anyway, in the 1980s rich donor nations started forgiving debts or reducing debts. Of the most heavily indebted countries, Father Christiansen points out, thirty-seven are in Africa and only four in Latin America.

All this gets very complicated. Father Christiansen leaves no doubt that there are monumental problems for poor countries, but canceling or reducing debt "is no panacea." Without economic growth through trade and development, nothing good is going to happen for poor people. One notes that in the now discredited theology of liberation, "development" was a dirty word, viewed as code language for entangling poor countries in a pattern of capitalist exploitation. But there is no alternative to development. "As now organized, international initiatives on debt will little affect Latin America's poor," according to Christiansen. "Debt reduction, new investment, and development will depend on the creation of an ethical environment in poor countries that penalizes corruption and promotes 'good government' practices, sound economic management, and dedicated work habits." Such a realistic assessment is not unanimously welcomed.

The sobriety of specificity is being reinforced even as we meet here. Each day the Italian press and *International Herald Tribune* are filled with lead stories on economic panic in Southeast Asia and South Korea. As the International Monetary Fund and other agencies scramble to find billions of dollars for massive bailouts of economies that were the great success story of recent decades but now teeter on the edge of catastrophe, it appears that there may not be much left over for canceling or significantly reducing the debts of countries that have not yet entered what *Centesimus Annus* calls "the circle of productivity and exchange."

Although it is not mentioned here, the burden of debt, internal and external, has burdened most Latin American nations ever since they gained their independence in the early nineteenth century. After independence, the federal government of the United States was also overwhelmed by debt. In 1790, the federal debt was $40.7 million domestic and $13.2 million foreign—enormous sums at the time. There seemed to be no way of repaying it until Alexander Hamilton, with the support of President Washington, created the fiscal and legal remedies for inflation and improvidence. This is one of many ways in which the United States had a good fortune denied to Latin America. It is very unfair, of course, and recalling this history does not solve the problems of indebtedness today, but a Church that thinks in terms of centuries should not forget that the problems of today were not created yesterday, or even twenty-five years ago.

The Circle of Productivity and Exchange

Notable among the interventions is that of Father Marcial Maciel, superior general of the Legionaries of Christ. Born in Mexico, Father Maciel launched the Legionaries as a young priest, and today, in a time when there is widespread lamentation about the lack of vocations to the priesthood, his movement has produced hundreds of priests and thousands of seminarians in the Americas and in Europe. Renewal movements such as the Legionaries—others are Opus Dei, Focolare, and the Neocatechumenal Way—are regularly described as "controversial," but have been strongly encouraged by John Paul II. The Legionaries are resented by some bishops, as new movements in the Church have been resented through the centuries. A particular complaint against the Legionaries is that they are too aggressive and "steal" both funding and priestly vocations from the dioceses, to which their answer is that they are generating funds and vocations that would otherwise not be available to the Church. My limited experience with the movement, both here and in the United States, leads me to think they are mostly right about that.

Among the synod fathers, Father Maciel is alone in lifting up the grass-roots potential for the creation of wealth. He describes a program in Mexico where well-to-do Catholics put up a hundred thousand dollars to be used in small loans to poor people who need a modest amount of capital to get started in business. Very modest indeed—typically a hundred or three hundred dollars to launch a small business in painting houses, marketing vegetables, or home-based manufacture of items for the tourist trade. After a few years of creatively circulating the capital fund, it has grown by leaps and bounds, and thirty-three thousand families have been helped to become economically self-sufficient, he reports. This program of "grass-roots capitalism" is hardly unique. In recent decades many North Americans have helped in establishing similar programs, and the British sociologist David Martin has studied the spread of such initiatives among evangelicals and pentecostalists in Latin America. The North–South "twinning" of Catholic parishes has resulted in thousands of such microeconomic ventures.

But Father Maciel's is the only intervention alluding to these entrepreneurial possibilities that are within the power of almost every bishop here. A concept that is at the heart of *Centesimus Annus* but seems to be almost totally ignored is "the subjectivity of society." The concept is deeply embedded in a Catholic anthropology—powerfully developed by Karol Wojtyla the philosopher before he became pope—of "the acting person" living in creative response to God's gracious creativity. It is a further extension of a phrase that Paul VI contributed to Catholic social doctrine, that persons should be "the artisans of their own destiny." Liberation theologians also emphasized that people should be the acting subjects and not simply the acted-upon objects of history, but they tended to tie that achievement to a revolutionary class struggle, a prospect that has been exposed as delusory. Unfortunately, the economic potential of "the subjectivity of society" does not come through in the *propositiones* issuing from the synod. One may hope that, too, will be remedied in the Holy Father's exhortation to America.

A different note is struck also by Professor Luis Meyer Jou, an auditor from Paraguay. In his little space of six minutes he proposes the big idea that the bishops are too resigned to the inevitability of Latin America being "an appendix to the U.S. supermarket." The economic experience of Brazil, Argentina, and Chile, he says, heralds the prospect of Latin America becoming a regional economic power comparable to the European Union. He refers approvingly to Archbishop Francis George's insight about the Protestantism of North American culture and suggests that the question is whether the economic potential of Latin America will be realized under Catholic or Protestant auspices. The professor offers a dramatic challenge to both the tone and substance of innumerable other interventions, but in the course of the synod nobody picks up on it, which is a pity. Even in some of the more strident criticisms of America's "neoliberal" hegemony—no, especially in the more strident criticisms—the underlying assumption is that Latin Americans are the objects of a history determined by others. Both Father Maciel and Professor Meyer propose alternatives which one must hope will get a better hearing in the future than they are apparently receiving here.

The Push and Pull of Immigration

The resignation to continuing dependence on the American hegemony is glaringly evident in the many interventions dealing with immigration. It seems to be simply assumed that there will be, for as long as one can see into the future, millions of Latin Americans heading North in search of economic opportunity. The further assumption is that the North, meaning chiefly the United States, has an obligation to receive and care for such immigrants. In this connection, at least two bishops cite St. Paul's affirmation in Galatians 3:28: "There is neither Jew nor Greek, there is neither slave nor free, there is neither male nor female; for you are all one in Christ Jesus"—adding that there is neither North or South. In the life of the Church that is certainly true, but this is an odd application of an ecclesiological truth to the question of national borders.

The editorial position of the *Wall Street Journal*, intended to be provocative, is in favor of a constitutional amendment to abolish America's borders. The purpose is both to provide economic opportunity to millions of immigrants and to assure an ample labor supply in the United States. A good, if not entirely persuasive, argument can be made for the position of the *Wall Street Journal*, but one may wonder if that should the position of the Catholic Church. The Church is universal; nations, by definition, are not. Nobody here at the synod is explicitly calling for the abolition of national borders, but neither is anybody challenging the suggestion that there is something inherently unjust in America's efforts to control its borders. Were the question pressed, I have no doubt that many bishops, both North and South, would challenge that suggestion.

But reticence is the rule here when it comes to anything touching on minority sensibilities, and maybe that's the way it should be. There is a line, however, between reticence and self-denigration. Monsignor Dennis Schnurr, general secretary of the U.S. bishops' conference, speaks about *e pluribus unum*, which means, he says, that the United States should become a glorious mosaic. "With sadness we view how we have treated indigenous peoples and those who are newly arrived," he says. The Indian question and African slavery are separate cases, but does America really have reason to apologize for its treatment of the many millions of immigrants from Europe, Asia, and Latin America? Historically and still today, the United States receives more voluntary immigrants than the rest of the world combined. America is a success story in the same way a Broadway play is declared a success: people are lined up around the block wanting to get in. Of course many immigrants have a hard time and the Church must do what it can to help them, but for the people involved the hard time is obviously worth it to gain access to what they perceive as the opportunities of living in America.

Students of immigration policy talk about a "push-pull" dynamic. People are pushed from their own countries by poverty and a lack of opportunity, and pulled to the United States by relative wealth and abundance of opportunity. With a few exceptions, the synod fathers appear to believe that the existing push-pull factor is a permanent feature of relations between North and South. Especially but not exclusively in Latin American interventions, the premise is that economics is a zero-sum game: the poor are poor because the rich are rich. In one general session, an American archbishop flatly declares to the bishops of the South, "We enjoy enormous economic resources that we rightly owe to you." One has to wonder what that means, since he is apparently talking not about the Church in the United States but about the wealth of the United States itself.

The Promise of Globalization

A very different tack is taken by Edmund Cardinal Szoka. He is the former archbishop of Detroit and something of a hero in curial circles.

In recent years he has been in charge of the Holy See's budget and has managed to pull it out of the deep red and into solvency. The press regularly describes this achievement as helping the Holy See to "turn a profit," which is hardly the case. But the Holy See has been able to pay its bills for several years running, and Szoka has more recently been elevated to the position of governor of Vatican City, in which he also maintains an oversight of finances. With utmost politeness, Cardinal Szoka indicates his impatience with the many depictions of "globalization" as the bogey-man of world economics.

Globalization, he says, is probably inevitable. He is not entirely sure what the term means, nor does he think others are. The more he deals with economic matters, and the more he talks with expert economists, the more he is persuaded "that nobody really understands economics, which has dynamics of its own." The one thing he is sure of is that God is still in charge, "and God can also use this phenomenon called globalization." Szoka quotes the line of Charles Peguy, "God writes straight with crooked lines." Far from being afraid of globalization, should not the Church, which is itself global in nature and vision, welcome the possibilities that may be inherent in economic dynamics that bring peoples and nations together? He proposes, "Also through economics, God may be moving us toward a fuller understanding that we are one world, one brotherhood of mankind." I don't know how many he is persuading, but the cardinal has the close attention of the synod fathers. He concludes his intervention by quoting a prayer by Rabbi Abraham Joshua Heschel that we may have the wisdom to discern God's purposes in the small piece of time that is ours.

The Church understands itself to be the presence through time of the One who is the Lord of time; as such, it is itself very much "timed." To be sure, it bears truths that are eternal and even the One who is Truth himself. The Church is also the gathering of the heirs of the apostles, with Peter among them, on a specific day in December in an overheated aula at the end of a century that has loosed rivers of blood and heaped up mountains of corpses in the name of ideologies that claimed to have the answer for the dissatisfactions of the human condition, the most devastating of such ideologies teaching a doctrine of economic determinism. Get the economic factor right, Marxist-Leninism claimed, and everything else will fall into place, issuing in a kingdom of freedom and equality.

Although it is only a few short years since the evil empire based on that doctrine collapsed—and everyone can now agree that it was indeed an evil empire—the awareness of that history is seldom in evidence in this synod. There is something curiously ahistorical about many of the interventions and discussions. A Latin American bishop who was a vigorous opponent of liberation theology when it was riding high has his own explanation for what is happening. The ideology of class struggle, he says, is still very much with us. He tells me that much of the rhetoric of resentment against the North is in fact code language for unreconstructed liberation theology based on, as they used to say, "Marxist analysis." Maybe he is right, but it doesn't feel that way to me. Even some of the more strident attacks on neoliberalism (now "so-called neoliberalism") reflect less a sense of ideological aggressiveness and more a sense of simply being at a loss.

I expect few of these Latin American bishops were ever strong proponents of liberation theology. One does not become a bishop, at least not ordinarily, by espousing revolution. But many of them may have imbibed a basic understanding of economics in terms of class struggle. The plausibility of that view is reinforced in countries where a small oligarchy has for generations possessed the great bulk of the land and other material resources, while most of the population hovers at the edges in wretched poverty. Marxist analysis provided one explanation of why this is the case. That explanation, at least in its overtly Marxist form, is now discredited. In the minds of many Latin Americans, one explanation is dead but another is still waiting to be born.

A Choice of Capitalisms

A new and more convincing explanation has in fact been articulated in the social teaching of this pontificate. The problem of poverty, according to the 1991 encyclical *Centesimus Annus*, is not, as Marx claimed, to be explained in terms of the exploitation of the poor by the rich. The problem is not so much exploitation as marginalization; the poor are those who have, for whatever reasons, not been included in the circle of productivity and exchange. In some cases they have been excluded, in others they have excluded themselves, in yet others they have not been invited. *Centesimus Annus* is keenly attuned to history, or, as the Second Vatican Council put it, to "reading the signs of the times." This is not surprising in view of the fact that it is written by a pope who lived through the alternatives to freedom in both their Nazi and Communist versions. He is also a philosopher of the phenomenology of human action as the source of creativity in response to the creativity of God. This explanation of the way the world works has very practical implications for economic activity that is premised upon "the subjectivity of society."

History does not usually give us the choices we would prefer. As Cardinal Szoka notes, some things are presented to us with the force of being inevitable. That captures also the spirit of *Centesimus Annus* when it asks the question, "Is capitalism the model which ought to be proposed to the countries of the Third World that are searching for the path to true economic and civil progress?" The pope's response to that question bears close examination:

> The answer is obviously complex. If by "capitalism" is meant an economic system that recognizes the fundamental and positive role of business, the market, private property, and the resulting responsibility for the means of production, as well as free human creativity in the economic sector, then the answer is certainly in the affirmative, even though it would perhaps be more appropriate to speak of a "business economy," "market economy," or simply "free economy." But if by "capitalism" is meant a system in which freedom in the economic sector is not circumscribed within a strong juridical framework which places it at the service of human freedom in its totality and sees it as a particular aspect of that freedom, the core of which is ethical and religious, then the reply is certainly negative.

The reply is certainly negative if by "capitalism" one means a situation such as that of Ciudad del Este, Paraguay. Situated on the border of Brazil, Ciudad del Este is sometimes compared to Hong Kong in its pre-communist days of bullish free enterprise. The difference is that Ciudad del Este is run by gangsters and drug lords, and 90 percent of the products it sells are counterfeits assembled from parts imported illegally from Taiwan and China. A bishop tells me that every month two thousand pounds of cocaine pass through Ciudad del Este on the way to Brazil, the United States, and Europe. The police are in the pay of the smugglers and drug traffickers and therefore stand passively by.

If they did crack down on illegal activity, the six hundred thousand people who depend upon the economy of Ciudad del Este would go hungry the next day. "You must understand," says the bishop, "that we, too, have some experience with capitalism."

The choice, it would seem, is between two capitalisms. The capitalism that is certainly to be affirmed is largely, albeit very imperfectly, the economic reality of North America. The "capitalism" of South America—as also in some post-Communist countries of Eastern Europe—is the freedom of a few, and of transnational actors, that is not contained by a juridical framework that directs freedom to the common good. Again, such a generalization must be qualified by the significant differences among Latin American countries, a qualification that has frequently surfaced during this synod. As important as a framework of laws and political accountability is a culture attuned to freedom and responsibility. The alternative is a culture of dependency. People must believe that they can be the subjects and not the objects of history, that they can be, in the words of Paul VI, the artisans of their own destiny.

The Church, if it specializes in anything, specializes in what people believe. The Church is uniquely positioned to inculcate the ethos, the practices, and the expectations of what John Paul II calls "the free economy." What the Catholic Church can do to change the practices of the International Monetary Fund or transnational corporations is painfully limited, even if we knew what changes would really benefit the poor, which is by no means certain. What the Catholic Church can do to cultivate attitudes and practices supportive of economic enterprise is immense. Many years ago, Max Weber wrote about the connections between capitalism and "the Protestant ethic," and observers today note that Protestant missionary activity in Latin America is typically accompanied by a dramatic increase in economic enterprise.

The link between culture and economics keeps cropping up in interventions by the synod fathers. Bishops from both North and South have said that the Catholic culture of Latin America is superior in its capacity to help people cope with deprivation, suffering, and death, and there is probably truth in that. The other side of this truth is that a culture disposed toward freedom, opportunity, and success is viewed as suspiciously "Protestant." No doubt there is in North America a style of individualistic boosterism, self-reliance, and "positive thinking" that is profoundly alien to the Catholic spirit. We have to believe, however, that the choice is not between unbridled individualism and communal solidarity, between enterprise and passivity, between freedom and hopeless dependence. St. Paul says to the Corinthians, "I will show you a more excellent way," and that, I believe, is what we are being told in Catholic social teaching, and most particularly in *Centesimus Annus*. After listening to these hundreds of speeches, one has the distinct impression that, in the important sphere of life we call economic, relatively few bishops in the North or the South have grasped the promise of that more excellent way.

5

In Search of a Great Awakening

Understanding a Hostile Culture That, All-unknowing, Hungers for Holiness

T HE HISTORY OF THE UNITED STATES is often told in terms of Great Awakenings. Historians are not agreed on how many such Great Awakenings there have been. There is no doubt about the Great Awakening in the first part of the eighteenth century, which produced the spiritual energy and heightened sense of communal self-confidence that made possible—some say inevitable—the revolt against British rule. Nor is there much disagreement about the Great Awakening of the nineteenth century that began with revivalistic eruptions in the frontier hinterlands and ended up by taming cities made turbulent by industry and immigration, launching a worldwide missionary crusade, and building a "benevolent empire" of charities and social services attending to almost every conceivable human need. It also produced, by no means incidentally, the grandly flawed experiment of the prohibition of alcohol. Some historians count as a third Great Awakening the rise of the liberal "social gospel" movement and the accommodation of Christianity to the bundle of ideas gathered under the title of "modernism."

Those who in the first part of this century were called, and called themselves, fundamentalists condemned that last development, which they viewed not as a Great Awakening but as the Great Defection. Their heirs today, broadly known as evangelicals, are now poised for another Great Awakening. Sometimes their expectation is joined to apocalyptic predictions of the end of history, and sometimes to a triumphal march toward "winning the world for Christ." This way of

86

thinking about Great Awakenings is emphatically American and emphatically Protestant. It is inseparably linked to the "enthusiasm" that Monsignor Ronald Knox so devastatingly criticized in his book by that title as the very antithesis of the Catholic way of being Christian. And yet, although they are not usually called Great Awakenings, periods of powerful spiritual resurgence are hardly foreign to Catholic history. One thinks of the great monastic renewals of the Middle Ages or of the seventeenth- and eighteenth-century Counter-Reformation (some prefer "Catholic Reformation") spear-headed by the Jesuits.

Then there is the grand vision projected by the Constitution on the Church in the Modern World (*Gaudium et Spes*, "Joy and Hope") of the Second Vatican Council. John Paul II, then archbishop of Krakow, was closely involved in the writing and adoption of *Gaudium et Spes*. When he is now asked whether, in view of what has happened since, that document was not somewhat naive about an easy convergence between the gospel and the course of modernity, he allows that some council fathers may have been naive, but it was an "evangelical naiveté." No matter how many disappointments we encounter, the pope insists, the Church must never cease to bear witness to an "evangelical hope" for the human project itself, a project in which God has invested himself in Christ. In *Tertio Millennio Adveniente* and many other statements, John Paul has called the Church and the world to a heightened expectation of something like a Great Awakening.

This Synod for America is marked less by heightened expectation than by an almost wistful longing that some big thing might happen, something like a Great Awakening. The hundreds of speeches pick and probe at pieces of problem and promise, but only episodically is there a statement that raises a coherent vision of what might be, and then it is quickly swamped by another deluge of unrelated homilies, complaints, and exhortations to do—well, to do something. The code phrase for the something that is to be done is "the new evangelization." What that means was set forth with great care and persuasiveness in the 1991 encyclical *Redemptoris Missio* ("The Mission of the Redeemer"). One cannot suppress the thought that this synod is adding little to that encyclical and may, however inadvertently, be detracting from it. It is possible that I missed it, but I don't think there has been one reference to *Redemptoris Missio*, although the talk about evangelization has been numbingly incessant.

Getting the Gospel Straight

Part of the problem may be with the official theme of the synod, "Encounter with the Living Jesus Christ: The Way to Conversion, Communion, and Solidarity in America." That sounds great, but it does not parse very well. We have already heard Archbishops Cordes and George question the frequent confusions between "communion" and "solidarity." There is additional difficulty with the very order of the terms, implying that first one is converted, then one enters into communion with others who are converted, and then together we engage in the tasks mandated by solidarity. Although many bishops might be scandalized by the thought, that sequence reflects a typically Protestant way of understanding the Christian reality. Cardinal Ratzinger has noted on a number of occasions that for Catholics, unlike Protestants, conversion to Christ and conversion to the Church are one act of faith; *communio* is not something added to the new life in Christ, it *is* the new life in Christ.

On these questions I'm afraid that the opening address by the rapporteur, Juan Cardinal Sandoval Iniguez of Mexico, got us off on a shaky footing. He recalled the three goals given the synod by the Holy Father: the new evangelization, greater solidarity among the various churches, and shedding light on economic relations and other issues of justice. As we view the future of a continent that is "a multicolored mosaic," Sandoval says, we should do so with optimism and hope. We have "a great Christian and Catholic heritage to build on," and there is a history of martyrs and saints to inspire us. The new evangelization means revivifying all this through an "encounter with the living Christ." That encounter, he says, is "the great topic" of the synod. He goes on to say that the three key terms of the synod's theme—conversion, communion, and solidarity—are "three paths" leading to that encounter. But surely conversion, communion, and solidarity are not paths to the encounter with the living Jesus Christ. Each presupposes that encounter; indeed, each is an inseparable component of that encounter.

Cardinal Ratzinger, both in his general intervention and in the discussion of the synod message (*Nuntius*), tries to bring some clarity to this theological muddle. He hopes that the primary fruit of the synod will be a renewed catechesis about the encounter with the living Christ. That encounter is the conversion that encompasses communion and solidarity. The converted person lives in communion and lives out sol-idarity in a new life in which Christ is no longer "You" but "I." He cites St. Paul's words to the Galatians, a recurring passage in Ratzinger's writings, "It is no longer I who live but Christ who lives in me" (Gala-tians 2:20). In this understanding, evangelization is not something apart from, and is certainly not an escape from, the tasks of economic, political, and social justice. Evangelization is not the "spiritual" side of the equation, with such tasks being the real-world consequences. The pursuit of those tasks is delusory unless grounded in Christ. "The ques-tion is Christology," the Cardinal insists. "Christ is the true realism."

Ratzinger does not directly criticize the official theme of the synod, but the criticism of the way that theme is sometimes being construed is unmistakable. Cardinal Ratzinger is treated with great deference. He is one of the handful of participants who, when his name is announced as the next speaker, brings the assembly to full attention. (Except for the sleeping archbishop.) The pope perks up and is obviously listening with care. And then the other speeches resume. Within minutes of Ratzinger's intervention, a bishop is telling us that communion requires a reduction of the external debt imposed by neoliberalism and "a conversion of the economy to Christ." And so forth. One fears the new evangelization is not going to get very far without greater the-ological clarity about the meaning of evangelization.

Who Are These Bishops?

For the most part, however, these are not theologians, which may be just as well. However theologically muddled, there is no question that these bishops are deeply convinced of the truth and power of "the Catholic thing." They are intuitively possessed by what academic theologians call a "thick" ecclesiology—Christ, Our Lady, the saints and martyrs, the images, prayers, and miracles, the multitudes of the faithful in need of a shepherd and, above all, by the utter realism of the Mass. Their pas-toral practice and their sensibilities are, at least in many cases, much better than their formal theology. I find myself constantly returning to these questions: Who are these men? What sustains and drives them? No doubt, as in any gathering of human beings, some are mediocrities, men who stumbled on to the clerical path and kept going until one day it was decided that, in the absence of more promising candidates, they could be safely entrusted with the management of a local branch of the Catholic Church, Inc. That is human enough, and the Church, for whatever else it is, is certainly a human institution.

Allowing for all that, I keep coming back to the sense that these men know things that I don't know, bear burdens that I don't bear, and are possessed of a devotion to the Church that I envy. Impressed upon my mind is the answer when, at the ordination to priesthood, your name is called. I answered, and they answered, "I come to serve." I hope I have served, but always in ways that *I* have decided I could best serve, albeit with my bishop's blessing. These men are under orders in a way that I am not. Oddly enough, it seems they are more under orders the higher up they are in the hierarchy. The Holy Father most of all. They are locked in and thereby liberated by the transposition of the "I" in which they have no life apart from the life of Christ and his Church. It is admirable, and more than a little frightening.

For most of us there is a certain aura that surrounds bishops, archbishops, and cardinals—not to mention the pope. Although I suppose I have kept my inclination to deference in better check than most, one is ever mindful of the theological truth that these are the successors of the apostles. Imagine, two millennia later, the original twelve apostles multiplied four hundred times over, and I suppose they would look pretty much like the four thousand bishops of the Catholic Church. They would look pretty much like this aula-full of bishops talking, quibbling, praying, nodding off, and talking some more—and, throughout it all, there is a palpable yearning that something big might happen. Something like a Great Awakening.

Propaganda and Perspective

A great deal rides on what happens in the Americas. This is the reminder from Jozef Cardinal Tomko, one of the more commanding figures in the Roman Curia. He is prefect of the Congregation for the Evangelization of Peoples, formerly known as Propaganda Fide or the Congregation for the Propagation of the Faith. Established by Pius V in 1568 for missionary work in the Orient, Propaganda, as it is still commonly called, has one of the largest portfolios of the Roman dicasteries. Coordinating global evangelization, encouraging missionary vocations, establishing new churches, setting the boundaries of future dioceses, selecting their bishops, and organizing the distribution of moneys for missions, Tomko has the oversight of eighty-two missionary territories around the world.

He refuses to treat even the weaker churches of Latin America as dependents. Latin America, he says, has or will soon have half the Catholics in the world and should be producing half the missionaries for the world. Tomko is fully attuned to the prospect set forth in *Redemptoris Missio*, that the beginning of the third millennium should be "a springtime of world evangelization." At the same time, he is utterly sober about where that prospect is today. Like Roger Cardinal Etchegaray of the Pontifical Council for Justice and Peace in his intervention, Tomko suggests that America is the world's most vibrant center of Catholic life and mission, and therefore bears a singular responsibility for the coming of that hoped-for springtime.

The Church in Africa is rapidly growing, but is still only 14 percent of the population, Tomko says. And in Asia, where Propaganda had its most auspicious beginnings more than four centuries ago, less than 3 percent of the people are Catholic. Remove the Philippines and that figure falls to one-half of one percent. He doesn't mention it in the synod, but Tomko is key to the Church's strategy in relation to China. More than ten million Chinese Catholics are divided between an "underground church" that has undergone terrifying persecution for its loyalty to Rome and a "patriotic church" that has made its peace, although a sometimes troubled peace, with the regime. If and when China really opens up—and the view in Rome is that it is only a matter of time—it will create vast missionary possibilities, and the Church is determined not to repeat the mistakes of the seventeenth and eighteenth centuries when promising missions planted by Franciscans, Jesuits, and Dominicans came to sorrow over what is known as the "Chinese rites controversy." All the talk about "inculturation" today has strong missiological implications and reflects the concern that the gospel not be rejected because Christianity presents itself as something that is culturally alien and intrusive.

Tomko's reference to the Philippines touches on an intriguing phe-

nomenon. From my own parish in Manhattan to the remotest ends of
the earth (or so it seems), overseas Filipinos are a source of Catholic
vitality. In several conversations here, bishops talk about their own
experience of this. Some months ago I was speaking with a bishop
from a nominally Lutheran and overwhelmingly secular Scandinavian
country, and I asked whether there were signs of spiritual renewal in
his church. Oh yes, he answered, and proceeded to tell me about the
very lively Filipino community that has developed in recent years. They
seem to be a preternaturally Catholic people.

Youth Alive and Youth Indifferent

Signs of spiritual resurgence are not limited to Filipinos. The French
intellectual and confidant of Charles DeGaulle, Andre Malraux, said
shortly before he died in 1976, "The twenty-first century will be religious or it will not be at all." I'm not sure what Malraux meant by that,
for he said so many things, but the oft-quoted statement has the ring of
truth. "Spiritual hunger" is a phrase regularly used here at the synod,
especially with reference to young people. It alternates with assertions
that the youth of today are thoroughly secularized and spiritually indifferent. Some interventions include both statements, perhaps with justice. After all, no generation is all one thing or all the other. I think the
perception of a spiritual hunger has the upper hand, however, and I am
impressed by the frequency with which the World Youth Days are mentioned, and how in these events hundreds of thousands and even millions of young people respond with such excitement. Is it this pope, or
is it the papacy, or is it the gospel, or is it an inchoate reaction against
a decadent and life-emptying culture—or is it all of these combined?
Whatever it is, there are moments when the synod fathers smell springtime in the air. Just moments, however, before we return to the winter
of our discontents.

     In his private dining room, the pope had on display for a while
only one photograph, that of his helicopter descending amidst the
enormous crowds of young people at World Youth Day in Denver, Col-
orado. He speaks of that event with animation, and I expect it greatly
deepened his appreciation of the vitalities of the Church in the United
States. Many of the American bishops thought it would be a bust, that

American young people would not travel so far merely to listen to the pope and spend several days with him in prayer. But they came by the hundreds of thousands, and after the first day's encounter even a skeptical media reported with something approaching awe the ways in which a presumably secular and rebellious generation responded to John Paul's call to moral grandeur. And so it has been with other World Youth Days, most recently in Paris, where more than a million people, mainly young people, cheered and prayed at the final Mass.

Is this papal magic, or a sign that the generation coming into its own in the first decade of the new millennium is looking for something very different, maybe something like a Great Awakening? Here at the synod I keep a scorecard of the speeches, and one entry is marked "Youth." There is a column for "Indifference" and another for "Awakening," for interventions that are doleful and those that are hopeful. Two weeks into the synod and "Indifference" is ahead almost two to one. Bishop Donald Wuerl of Pittsburgh says the culture is pitted against young people. They grow up in a world that tells them that moral teaching cannot oblige the conscience, that everything is relative, that "the only truth is what is 'true for me.'" The great work of the synod, he urges, is to give birth to a new catechesis in the basics of the faith. Yet he ends on the note that today's youth are spiritually hungry, so his intervention gets a big check under "Indifference" and a small one under "Awakening."

Michael Bzdel, the Archbishop of the Ukrainian Rite in Winnipeg, Canada, manages in a few minutes to evoke a world that was, and that not so many years ago. It was the world of an intact immigrant community and a religious ethos so strong "that you could almost say young people grew up in a seminary." Now that is past, and it cannot be recreated. Then the Church's task was maintenance, he says, and now it must be evangelization. What used to be received by inheritance must now be appropriated by decision. He seems to think it can be done, so his intervention goes into the "Awakening" column. The auxiliary bishop of Sao Paulo, Brazil, Antonio Quieroz, is impatient with the naysayers. Why is there such a powerful response to the Holy Father? he asks. "Because he proclaims a hopeful vision of the world and its future, and because what he says is true." There it is again, the insistent theme of John Paul's 1978 inaugural sermon as pope: "Be not afraid!" And there are others who speak in a similar vein.

But there are many more speeches that call to mind Matthew

Arnold's reflections on "the sea of faith":

> But now I only hear
> Its melancholy, long, withdrawing roar
> Retreating, to the breath
> Of the night wind down the vast edges drear
> And naked shingles of the world.

One keeps in mind that bishops are, among other things, moralists, and moralists have the habit, and sometimes the duty, of warning that things are going to rack and ruin. A friend of conservative leanings sums up his credo in the simple proposition, "Change is bad." Some of the synod fathers appear to agree, while others are of a divided mind. A Brazilian bishop manages in the same intervention a ringing call for radical social change and an equally ringing denunciation of social dislocation, urbanization, and the "practical agnosticism" of today's youth. A more coherent response to change, and urbanization in particular, is proposed by Bishop Francisco Robles Ortega of Toluca, Mexico. While rapid urbanization has played havoc with traditional territorial parishes, he says, they can still provide the framework for evangelization and effective pastoral care. The key is the redeployment of base communities, or *comunidades eclesiales de base*.

Base Communities and the Communio of the Church

The same idea is pressed by Bishop Fernando Lugo of Paraguay, who calls base communities the motor of the new evangelization—*el motor de la nueva evangelizacion*. While they are not unknown in Africa and Asia, base communities have been especially prominent in Latin America. In part, they grew up in response to a severe shortage of priests. More positively, they are initiatives led by the laity to create small groups centered in scripture study, prayer, and mutual support in living the Christian life. Nobody seems to know exactly how many, but there are certainly thousands of *comunidades eclesiales de base* throughout Latin America. Paul VI encouraged them as an instrument of evangelization in a 1975 apostolic exhortation, *Evangelii Nuntiandi*, as they had also been endorsed by the Medellin, Colombia, meeting of the Conference of Latin American Bishops (CELAM) in 1968. The

Medellin conference also ringingly affirmed "the preferential option for the poor," and was for years celebrated as the moment in which the Church in Latin America formally ratified the revolutionary vision of liberation theology.

The growth of base communities has not been without controversy. All three words in "basic ecclesial communities" are important. They are basic in that they involve people at the "base" of the Church's structure, and in that they address the basics of everyday life. They are ecclesial in that they are part of the *communio* that holds the Church together in one faith and one allegiance. And they are communities in that they strive to counter the individualizing and fragmenting dynamics of the modern world. By the time of the CELAM conference held in Puebla, Mexico, in 1979, many bishops had misgivings that base communities were becoming "parallel churches" in competition with the "official church," and the conference called for closer bonds with the local churches and their bishops. In the middle of the 1980s, the Congregation for the Doctrine of the Faith (CDF) issued two "instructions" that were sharply critical of Marxist liberationism and, or so some thought, base communities.

Prominent liberation theologians such as Juan Luis Segundo and Leonardo Boff contended that their liberation theology employed "Marxist analysis" but that did not make it ideologically Marxist. Rome took the position also taken by almost all Marxist theorists, that Marxist theory and *praxis* are fundamentally incompatible with Christianity in, among other things, their understanding of anthropology, the determinants of human action, and the limits of history. The more radical proponents of liberation theology met with opposition not only from the bishops and from Rome, however. They had tied the liberationist project to a number of revolutionary programs in Latin America that turned out to be disastrous. Most notable was the Sandinista government led by Daniel Ortega in Nicaragua, in which several liberationist priests served as ministers, against the explicit orders of church superiors. Before the Sandinistas were repudiated in 1990 by free elections, they had discredited their cause by heavy-handed opposition to the Church, including an orchestrated effort to embarrass John Paul II on a pastoral visit to the country. Wounding also were undeniable revelations about the corruptions, both petty and grand, of the Sandinistas while in power.

Some liberation theologians blamed U.S. policy under Ronald Reagan for what had gone wrong with the Nicaraguan revolution; others tried to distance their own position from the Sandinista experiment, but by the time the Latin American bishops met in 1992 at Santo Domingo, in the Dominican Republic, liberation theology was under a very heavy cloud. Its proponents seized upon a 1986 letter to the Brazilian bishops in which the pope allowed that, once it had been purified of Marxist and other alien elements, liberation theology could be "legitimate and necessary," but that was slight consolation. Both censures from Rome and unhappy historical experience had taken their toll, but this gave the bishops at Santo Domingo the opportunity to sort out what could be salvaged from the liberationist project. They again affirmed the *comunidades eclesiales de base*, some of them arguing that the phenomenon of base communities had only been temporarily hijacked by liberation theology. That is an argument pressed also by leaders of lay renewal movements who insist that they had been working with base communities long before liberation theology came along and tried to politicize them.

Here at the synod one bishop makes a rhetorically impressive appeal that this meeting should be seen in continuity with Medellin, Puebla, and Santo Domingo. "It will be a success if it is seen as Medellin IV." That does not seem to have many takers. A Mexican bishop remarks in conversation, "Medellin is something past. Of course it is all part of the experience of the one Church, but we have learned a great deal since Medellin. We can't have a 'new evangelization' if we keep going back and repeating our mistakes." Quite apart from ideological disputes, it would seem that base communities must be a major part of the Church's strategy in Latin America, if for no other reason than the severe shortage of priests. Even if there were no priest shortage, however, others insist that base communities are a permanent feature of the Church's life. There is so much to be done. they say, that every potential resource must be employed.

It is to such realities on the ground, so to speak, that Bishop Romulo Emiliani of Panama directs our attention in his intervention. "We must focus on our own failures," he declares. It is all very well to call for grand changes in the name of the preferential option for the poor, he suggests, but the real tasks are closer to hand. "We must face the fact that shanty towns, jails, alleys, and abortion clinics are the real

option for the poor." Nothing will help now but hard everyday coop-
erative work by bishops, priests, and lay people. As for all the
expressed concern about Protestant proselytizing, "The more we do
our job, the less room there will be for the sects."

Media and Higher Education in a Hostile Culture

According to Archbishop Larrea Holguin of Ecuador, the media, and
television in particular, are the enemy of the new evangelization. Not
surprisingly, he deplores violence and pornography. If I understand
him correctly, the remedy is television that is free from "the pressure of
advertisers." He is not alone in seeing the sinister hand of neoliberalism
behind the threat of the media, and most who speak on the subject do
view the media as a threat. The "sects" use the media, especially radio,
very successfully, says Bishop Sarasti Jaramillo of Colombia, but that is
because they are supplied with a deluge of dollars from the North.

The leader of the Canadian delegation, the imposing Jean-Claude
Cardinal Turcotte of Montreal, weighs in most heavily on the media.
We are caught up in a media revolution, it seems, that is changing
human consciousness and making it almost impossible for the Church
to communicate its message. There are a few interventions suggesting
that Catholics are tempted to blame the media because they are inept
at using it, and there is at least one oblique reference to the great success of Mother Angelica's Eternal Word Television Network as something that might be emulated, but these interventions are in the
distinct minority. The dominant view is that the media belong to
"them"—"them" meaning antireligious secularists and "the sects." One
cannot help but sympathize with the resentment of the globalization of
American popular culture through television, movies, and music. So
much of it is meretricious, but there is perhaps an inevitable connection between the tawdry and the popular.

The dominant note of the bishops, then, is that the culture is gen
erally, even aggressively, hostile to the new evangelization. Given the
vitalities of America, and especially of the United States, the tone is
not, as it is so often with Western Europeans, one of resignation to a
wearied, thoroughly secularized, and "post-Christian" culture. Rather,

the vitalities of America are perceived as being actively opposed to the Christian, especially the Catholic, mission. The many and ambivalent generalizations about the young tend to fit into this perception. In thinking about the next generation, one might expect that Catholic higher education would figure prominently in the synod's deliberations, but it receives surprisingly few references in the interventions. An exception is Father Kolvenbach, head of the Jesuits, who addresses the subject in some detail.

He speaks chiefly to the situation in the United States, where Jesuit schools such as Georgetown, Boston College, and Fordham are thought to be the elite institutions—along with non-Jesuit Notre Dame, of course—among more than two hundred Catholic colleges and universities. Almost all these schools were founded by religious orders such as the Jesuits, and following Vatican Council II there was a powerful move to enter into the "mainstream" of American higher education, breaking loose from what was thought to be the stifling limits of church control. In 1967, twenty-six heads of major institutions, with Father Theodore Hesburgh of Notre Dame presiding, issued the Land O'Lakes Statement. The opening paragraph declared: "To perform its teaching and research functions effectively the Catholic university must have a true autonomy and academic freedom in the face of authority of whatever kind, lay or clerical, external to the academic community itself."

"Autonomy" and "academic freedom"—especially academic freedom—quickly became the controlling mottoes as school after school hastened to liberate itself from "the Catholic ghetto" by means of "laicizing" or, as others more frankly said, "secularizing" their faculties, administrations, and boards of control. Many dynamics were in play apart from an envious emulation of prestigious schools such as those of the Ivy League and the desire to disprove the suspicion of cultural despisers of religion who viewed the term "Catholic university" as an oxymoron. A major factor, of course, was the rapid decline, in some cases a precipitous decline, in the number of members of religious orders available to staff these institutions. Nonetheless, some colleges and universities did in subsequent years attain a large measure of acceptance and respectability in the academic mainstream. Institutions such as Georgetown, Boston College, and Notre Dame are today recognized as research universities in the front ranks of American higher education. For these schools and their many lesser imitators, however, a steep price was paid in what is now commonly called "Catholic identity."

In many instances, bishops began to lose confidence in Catholic schools that seemed to be very doubtfully Catholic. Cutting closer to the bone of institutional survival, parents and alumni in large numbers began to wonder whether such schools offered an education that is, in any serious sense of the term, Catholic. In Rome, but also among many Catholic educators in the United States, the uneasiness grew that Catholic higher education was losing its way. By the mid-1980s, a feeling had grown that there was something very much like a crisis in Catholic higher education. Scholars urged that, unless something was done and done quickly, Catholic colleges and universities would go the way of Harvard, Yale, Princeton, Vanderbilt, and other elite institutions that had long lost touch with the Christian inspiration that had brought them into being. Not surprisingly, many others in Catholic higher education thought that going the way of schools such as Harvard and Yale was precisely the goal.

This was the circumstance in which the Vatican issued in 1990 an apostolic constitution on higher education, *Ex Corde Ecclesiae* ("From the Heart of the Church"). As the title suggests, the document was a call to renew and reconstitute the bonds between Church and academy. While it has greatly heightened concern about "Catholic identity," *Ex Corde Ecclesiae* has by no means reversed the direction set by the manifesto of Land O'Lakes. Many champions of that direction loudly protested what they claimed was the constitution's effort to reimpose stifling restrictions, while others thought they could negotiate their peace with it. Those who believe Catholic higher education has lost, or is losing, its way claim that such champions are clearly evading the mandates of the document, especially when it comes to making sure that their institutions are teaching authentically Catholic theology and morality. This is the circumstance addressed by Father Kolvenbach, with specific reference to Jesuit colleges and universities, of which there are at present twenty-eight in the United States.

In his intervention, Father Kolvenbach manages to pack in some of the history recounted above, and notes that the relationship between academic freedom and ecclesial allegiance continues to be "problematic." Too often, he says, academic freedom means that all voices are equal, except the voice of the Church. Affirmative action is employed to make sure that all kinds of groups and viewpoints are represented, and he suggests that it may be time for an affirmative action program in favor of Catholics who care about the Catholic character of the institutions. He stresses the complexity of difficulties created by factors both internal and external to the university, and declares that the Society of Jesus will continue to work on these difficulties in order to realize the vision of *Ex Corde Ecclesiae*. After he finished speaking, some bishops expressed puzzlement as to exactly what had been said.

In my interviews with Father Kolvenbach over the years, he has been refreshingly candid in his response to questions. He is a gentle and unassuming man, in his mid-sixties I should think, and utterly unpretentious. Unlike many churchmen in high positions, his answers never seem canned but are genuinely responsive to the questions posed. As to what he meant to say about Jesuit higher education, he answers that "for some universities, it is probably too late to restore their Catholic character." One has to ask what a few Jesuits can do in a university when eighty percent of the faculty is not even Catholic, and most of them don't care or don't like the idea of the institution being Catholic. Moreover, it can hardly be taken for granted that the twenty percent that is Catholic either understands or wants what is required to be a Catholic institution. An additional factor, he says, is that schools have handed over control to boards of laymen who are not always Catholic and frequently do not understand the meaning of a Jesuit university. When control was transferred, there were charters that were supposed to guarantee the Jesuit character of the schools in perpetuity. But once religious orders have lost real control, smart lawyers can find ways of interpreting charters the way they want and there is not much to be done about it. This is a grim view of the future of Catholic, or at least of Jesuit, higher education.

As Father Kolvenbach is personally unassuming, he is also unassuming about the Society of Jesus. He is so straightforward and candid that the thought once occurred to me that he is being crafty, in the sense that once gave a sinister connotation to the word "Jesuitical." But that was centuries ago, and I do not believe it for a minute of Father Kolvenbach. I have discussed with him the claim of critics who say that the Jesuits are no longer the order of militant fidelity that Ignatius Loyola established four centuries ago, that maybe the order has outlived its usefulness. Those who take this view cite the steep decline in

Jesuit numbers and influence, plus more recent tensions with the papal authority the order was established to champion. Father Kolvenbach is most amiably unfazed by this line of inquiry, allowing that there are very few "permanent charisms" in the Church. The charism, or founding inspiration, of the Benedictines and of the Franciscans is probably permanent in the sense of being necessary to the Church, he opines. But if the time has run out for the Jesuit charism, he says, that poses no great crisis. "Ignatius said from the beginning that, if the time ever came when we were not needed, we would immediately disband." No Jesuit, he adds, should be disturbed by the possibility that that time has come. Of course he does not say that is the case. It is a great tribute to the Society of Jesus, or at least to its history, that so many renewal movements that have emerged in recent years admit, at least *sotto voce*, that they aspire to being "the new Jesuits."

Evangelizing through Holiness

The synod fathers refer frequently to such renewal movements, although never by name. The usual phrase is "lay movements," and it is obvious that a great deal of hope is pinned on them. Interventions become more animated at the mention of these eruptions of holiness, despite the generally doleful depiction of our cultural circumstance. I think it fair to say that the bishops evidence more confidence in the surprises of the Holy Spirit than in their capacity to reform declining institutions. Brazzini Diaz-Ufano of Lima, Peru, for instance, in one of the few references to higher education other than Kolvenbach's, talks about what a great difference it would make if Catholic colleges and universities were really Catholic. But the gist of his message is that nothing will make a difference without holiness. "The first evangelization of America was marked by sanctity," he declares. "Can that truly be said of us who now talk about a new evangelization?"

Mexico's Alberto Suarez India presses the point: "The credibility of Christ passes through his priests. He said, 'He who hears you hears me,' but to hear Christ they must see him in us and through us. The best evangelizer is the saint." The Archbishop of Santo Domingo with the marvelous name of Nicolas de Jesus Lopez Rodriguez: "The only testimony that is credible is the testimony of those who know the Lord. The unconverted cannot believably call to conversion." He adds that priests must be formed so that they preach the *kerygma*—the core content of the gospel in the life, death, resurrection, and coming again of Jesus the Christ. Brazil's Claudio Hummes suggests that we have lost our nerve to really challenge young people, and he cites the electric response to John Paul II on his recent visit to Rio de Janiero when he declared to the youth, "God calls you to holiness. He loves you madly." As I listen to Archbishop Hummes, I am reminded of a priest in Poland who has known the pope for many years, and he tells me that the secret of his attraction is that everything he says is a variation on one theme: "You are capable of ever so much more than you think. God calls you to spiritual and moral grandeur."

In this vein, the auxiliary bishop of San Salvador, Gregorio Rosa Chavez, speaks movingly of his former archbishop, Oscar Romero, who was assassinated while celebrating Mass on March 24, 1980. Romero spoke out boldly for human rights and the poor during a time of great political turmoil in El Salvador. While some thought him too political and uncritically sympathetic to liberation theology, he is today widely revered as a martyr. True holiness, says the bishop, is a readiness to lay down our lives for others, and he cites Jesus on the seed bearing no fruit unless it falls into the ground and dies. Although he does not cite the passage, I am surely not alone in being reminded of the words of the second-century Tertullian, "The blood of the martyrs is the seed of the Church."

Saints come one by one, but their holiness is corporate. In the Mass, just before the *Agnus Dei,* the priest prays, "Look not on our sins but on the faith of your Church." And on the way others have lived the faith so much better than we. Much of the holiness of the Church is anonymous, as is the Latin American bishop who made a striking intervention in this connection. As he began to speak the television monitors went on the blink, nobody around me knew who was speaking, and there is no transcript (except, I suppose, in the vaults of the Synod of Bishops). But what he said was memorable. All holiness begins with the forgiveness of sins purchased by the blood of Christ, he said, and his devotion to us elicits devotion from us. The bishop noted that an unprecedented number of saints have been canonized during this pontificate, and he had a practical suggestion. Instead of just ringing the bells of St. Peter's when a saint is canonized, there should be a rule that bells are to be rung all over the world at the same time. Doing it at the same time may be a problem, since in much of the world that would mean ringing bells in the middle of the night, but it is an undeniably attractive idea.

To Be the Salt of the Earth

Those who think renewal can be brought about by better techniques of management or communication, and those who measure the Church's effectiveness in terms of economic and political influence, cannot help but be skeptical about all this talk about holiness. An Italian journalist writes of the second week of the synod: "Many of the synod fathers are trying to change the subject from the hard work of justice in this world and the hard problems of an outdated message by escaping into the discussion of spiritual questions." A very different understanding of the Church and its mission is proposed by Cardinal Ratzinger in a new book-length interview, *The Salt of the Earth*, which I brought me with to the synod.

Ratzinger quotes an observation of the late Karl Rahner, a Jesuit and one of the most influential Catholic theologians of this century, "The Christian of tomorrow will be a mystic, or he will not be at all." Ratzinger reflects: "I would not ask for so much, because people are always the same. We always remain just as weak as ever, which means that we will not all become mystics. But Rahner is correct in that Christianity will be doomed to suffocation if we don't learn something of interiorization, in which faith sinks personally into the depth of one's own life and in that depth sustains and illuminates. Mere action and mere intellectual construction are not enough. It's very important that we recall simplicity and interiority and the extra- and supra-rational forms of perceiving reality." Everything turns on whether one thinks that is a counsel of "escape" or of renewal.

"The best evangelizer is the saint," says Alberto Suarez India of Mexico. Ratzinger agrees. Perhaps because he is so close to the dismally secularized and apparently post-Christian culture of Germany, and Western Europe more generally, Ratzinger tends to have a very sober, some might say somber, view of the Christian prospect in the years ahead. He sees a Church besieged, smaller in numbers, but, he hopes, more coherent and committed in faith. He well knows that only God knows what the future holds, but, whatever happens, everything turns on holiness. He puts it this way:

> The genuine reformers of the Church who have helped her to become simpler and at the same time to open a new access to salvation have always been the saints. Just think of Benedict, who, at the end of antiquity, created the form of life thanks to which the Church went through the great migrations. Or if you think of Francis and Dominic—in a feudalistic, ossifying Church, an evangelical movement that lived the poverty of the gospel, its simplicity, its joy, suddenly exploded and then unleashed a real mass movement. Or let's remember the sixteenth century. The Council of Trent was important, but it could be effective as a Catholic reform only because there were saints like Teresa of Avila, John of the Cross, Ignatius of Loyola, Charles Borromeo, and many others who were simply struck inwardly by the faith, who lived it with originality in their own way, created forms of it, which then made possible necessary, healing reforms. For this reason I would also say that in our time the reforms will definitely not come from forums and synods, though these have their legitimacy, sometimes even their necessity. Reforms will come from convincing personalities whom we may call saints.

No Substitute for Priests

Reforms will definitely not come from synods, the Cardinal says. But if there is to be a Great Awakening, also known as the new evangelization, perhaps synods can at least point to what stands in the way of that prospect. A good deal of discussion at this synod points to the shortage of priestly vocations, which is generally thought to be a "crisis," although there is not unanimous agreement on the nature of the crisis. Brazil's Bishop Angelico Sandalo Bernardino says there is one priest for every twenty thousand people in his country. Twenty thousand is the high figure; other countries report one priest for every five thousand, and it would seem the norm is around one priest for every ten thousand. By comparison, there is a priest for about every thousand Catholics in the United States.

In Brazil, the bishop says, only fifteen percent of the people are able to receive Communion on Sunday, while more than three million attend Sunday services that are led by lay people. The number of lay ministers—catechists, eucharistic ministers, and so forth—is growing rapidly, and the ratio is now seventy-five lay ministers to every ordained priest. The synod must ask, he says, "How can we provide a good solution to the problem of ordained ministers and their collaborators?" This and other interventions are suggesting, ever so gently, that the Church should rethink what is required on the route toward priestly ordination. One of the great reforms of the Council of Trent in the sixteenth century was the establishment of standardized seminary training for priests, and it is now obvious that at least some bishops in Latin America are wondering whether pastoral necessity is now forcing the Church to revisit that question.

Just as obviously, this synod is not ready to address that question directly. In addition to the shortage of priests, but closely related to the lack of pastoral care, is the fact that many Catholics are living in irregular marriages, says Bishop Nestor Rafael Herrera Heredia of Ecuador. These are often devout people, he says, who baptize their children, go to Mass, and try to live the Catholic life. He suggested that the synod should do something to make it possible for national episcopal conferences "to establish some rules, according to the situation of each country, that would make it possible for these people to receive the bread of life in the Eucharist." Perhaps in direct response to that suggestion, a few days later *L'Osservatore Romano*, which usually reflects the policy of the Holy See, explained why there should be no change in the norms for a valid marriage.

James Cardinal Hickey of Washington, D.C., was also concerned about priestly vocations and suggested that the problem might be related to the way priests are trained—or "priestly formation," as it is called. North and South, he said, should find new ways of cooperating so that priestly formation would prepare priests to minister throughout the Americas. "I like what he said," a Colombian bishop tells me afterward, "but I wonder if cooperation doesn't require more equality. The North has all the resources, and that means you have most of the responsibility." He and others report that in Latin America in recent years there has been a great increase in the number of men preparing for the priesthood, perhaps, he thinks, because a measure of political

stability is closing off career opportunities in the military. "Ten or fifteen years ago," he says, "many of the young men in our seminaries
would have been in the army." It is not only that the military is shrink-
ing in some places, he believes, but young men see the priesthood as a
more attractive opportunity for leadership than professional soldier-
ing. Nonetheless, he thinks it will be many years before Latin America
will even come close to having enough priests, and the prospect of
being able to supply priestly ministry to the millions who emigrate
North is nowhere on the horizon.

The view from Belo Horizonte, Brazil, is that the "crisis" of vocations in fact goes back to the 1970s, when so many who had been
ordained abandoned the priesthood. That, plus the fact that at about
the same time the idea gained ascendancy that missionary work is a
form of imperialism, and so hundreds of missionary priests returned
to the United States and Europe. Belo Horizonte's archbishop, Serafim
Fernandes de Araujo, adds that the growth of Protestant movements
has also contributed to the sense that things are increasingly out of
control. In 1991, he reports, only 83 percent of Brazil's population
identified themselves as Catholic, which does not necessarily mean
that they have fallen away from the faith. Less than one percent say
they do not believe in God, but many others are practicing what sociologist Thomas Luckman calls "invisible religion," meaning a religious
life disconnected from any community of faith. Despite that, the archbishop says that 30 percent of the Catholic population participates in
Sunday Mass. That would seem to be comparable to the United States,
where, depending on whose statistics you believe, 30 to 50 percent of
Catholics are said to participate in weekly Mass. Considering that Sunday Mass is for Catholics a solemn obligation, that may be viewed as a
crisis. On the other hand, compared with Western Europe, for
instance, 30 percent may be taken as a sign of a Church vibrantly alive.

Some interventions exhibit a robust skepticism toward the statistics that are being bounced around the aula. For instance, the intervention of a young bishop who raises some hackles. Speaking from his
own experience, rather than relying on the studies of putative experts,
he thinks the synod may be missing important and disturbing truths
about the men now being trained for the priesthood in Latin America.
"People who have not been evangelized," he says, "cannot be the agents
of the new evangelization." While there are more candidates for the

priesthood, many of them have not really been evangelized or converted. Then he declares flatly, "They are not Christians." He proposes that the synod set aside a holy hour before the Blessed Sacrament to pray for vocations, and for priests who are really Christians, so that Latin America can send them to the North and to Europe in order to convert the Church there. The assertion that many seminarians and young priests are not Christians catches the attention of synod fathers. A Brazilian archbishop says privately, "That was entirely out of order. I don't know what seminaries he knows. My seminarians are as devout as we were in seminary." Others think the young bishop may be on to something, but in the general sessions nobody responds directly to his description of the problem and what might be done about it.

My impression is that the archbishop of Bogota, Colombia, Pedro Rubiano Saenz, is impatient with what he views as excessive breast-beating about priestly vocations. He forcefully asserts that the only power the Church has is the power of love, and the attractiveness of the priesthood is "the scandal of love." If we scandalized the world with self-surrendering love, that would also be our greatest service to the common good of society. He says that too much of the synod has been about what is wrong with society and what we can do to change it. We should, he says, be asking the more radical question of "what we can be and what we can do as Church to demonstrate the scandal of Christian love." If we followed that course, there would be no shortage of priests. In fact, he doubts that there really is a shortage of priests. He suspects there may be a maldistribution of priests, but he knows there is a shortage of love. His is among the more invigorating interventions.

But the prize in that category goes to Mother Quentin Sheridan who is superior of a vibrant community, the Sisters of Mercy of Alma, Michigan, and secretary of the Council of Major Superiors of Women Religious. She uses her time to give the bishops a no-nonsense lecture on the dignity of their office. My goodness, she declares with a note of exasperation, "The priest acts *in persona Christi!*"—in the person of Christ. It is a well-crafted speech by a formidable woman who seems more than a little put out that she has to remind bishops and priests of who they are. Implicit in her remarks is that it is unseemly for synod fathers to be devoting so much time to complaining, even whining, about the difficulties they face. Her message, in effect, is, "Get on with the job God has given you!" The only crisis of the priesthood, she lets us know, is the crisis of priests and bishops who don't understand the immeasurable gift and task that is theirs. Her intervention is a nice mix of maternal affirmation and reproach, and the bishops, both flattered and abashed, respond with warm applause.

A Call to Action and a Call to Prayer

If there is to be a new evangelization, a spiritually awakened clergy is no doubt greatly to be desired, but we have been told that the best evangelizer is the saint, and all one billion Catholics in the world are called to be that. The only reason for the existence of the clergy is to help the People of God (one of Vatican II's favored terms for the Church) be what they are called to be. It is to the entire Church that 1 Peter 2:9 declares, "You are a chosen race, a royal priesthood, a holy nation, God's own people, that you may declare the wonderful deeds of him who called you out of darkness into his marvelous light." Recall again John Henry Cardinal Newman's answer when he was asked what he thought of the laity: "We would look pretty silly without them, wouldn't we?"

The idea of mobilizing the laity for the great cause of renewal is hardly new. But there is something skewed in the notion that the laity should be mobilized by the clergy. Justin Rigali, archbishop of St Louis, Missouri, touches on a historical instance of this in his intervention. He refers to the "Call to Action" conference of 1976 that the U.S. bishops convened in Detroit, which brought together thousands of laity with high hopes of ushering in a period of great renewal in accord with the vision of the Second Vatican Council that was concluded a decade earlier. Many bishops hoped that Detroit would lay the groundwork for a restructuring of Catholic leadership, with permanent provisions for the laity in the making of important decisions. After the fact, it was generally recognized that Detroit was something of a fiasco and a severe setback to the cause of the laity.

Numerous interest groups poured into Detroit to capture the Church's influence and resources for their sundry purposes, usually left-leaning causes of social change. Moreover, since the event had been convened by clerical leadership, the question of clerical leadership loomed large in the conference's debates and agitations. The bishops soon found themselves very much on the defensive, faced by demands for the "democratization" of the Church from top to bottom, for a repudiation of the Church's teaching on contraception as it had been reaffirmed in the much-controverted 1968 encyclical *Humanae Vitae*, and for much else that the bishops could not deliver even if some of them might have wanted to. The slogan at the time on the radical edges of American society was "Power to the People!" and Detroit echoed that in its version of the laity as the People of God. Clerical calls to action can elicit a very active anticlericalism, which of course is another form of clericalism. Both clericalism and anti-clericalism tend to see the Church chiefly in terms of the clergy, and end up focusing energies *ad intra*—on internal power relationships—rather than *ad extra* — as in a new evangelization of the world.

This was the background of Archbishop Rigali's caution that the synod not see itself, or at least not see itself chiefly, as a call to action. He cited a letter from Paul VI that was read at the opening session of the Detroit conference. "A call to action," said the pope, "must begin with a call to prayer." Like many others here, Rigali wants to turn the synod's attention to holiness, without which structural rearrangements and agitations for social and economic change are empty gestures. Only through earnest prayer will the many gifts of the Spirit, meaning mainly gifts given the laity, be stirred to service for both Church and world. Although he and others do not say so explicitly, he and other synod fathers may well have in mind the recent instruction from eight dicasteries setting out the limits of lay participation in liturgical roles traditionally reserved to the clergy. There is additional ambiguity in the synod's discussion of the laity because of the frequent references to the laity taking up the slack, so to speak, created by the severe shortage of priests, especially in Latin America. All of this reinforces the notion of the laity as an appendix to the clergy, who constitute the core reality that is the Church. A long-standing complaint among Catholics is that lay people are viewed as "Father's little helper." Where there is no priest, as one bishop put it privately, "Father's little helper" becomes "Father's little substitute."

Archbishop Daniel Pilarczyk of Cincinnati intervenes on the question of lay ministry. "Lay persons contribute in precious ways to the mission of the Church," he says. He goes on to note that in the United

States there are more than thirty thousand lay ministers who are financially compensated in one way or another, which does not seem so many if it includes all the parishes and schools with their music directors, sextons, secretaries, and so forth. He suggests that more care should be taken with "ecclesial lay ministers" in making sure they are properly certified and recognized. A good point no doubt, but there is a danger of a limited view of lay ministry that confines it to "church work" rather than encompassing all that is entailed in the Church at work in the world. The archbishop of Paraiba, Brazil, Marcelo Pinto Carvalheira, seeks to counter that danger with a caution against "clericalizing the laity." Lay people contribute to the mission of the Church, but much more importantly they *are* the mission of the Church. Remembering this, the archbishop suggests, will be critically important as the institutions of the Church become even more dependent on lay leadership.

Those "Controversial" Renewal Movements

While there are numerous references to "renewal movements" in the Church, they are not mentioned by name. Perhaps that is because bishops do not want to play favorites among the several movements, or because some of these movements are deemed to be "controversial"— controversy being the frequent companion of authentic renewal. I have already mentioned the Legionaries of Christ, founded by the Mexican priest Father Maciel, who in the aula has the seat to my left. Although established chiefly for priestly vocations, the Legionaries also have a lay organization, Regnum Christi, in which thousands of lay people deepen their discipleship precisely as lay people. Although they come in for the usual criticisms, there is nothing besieged or sweated about the Legionaries. Events with their seminarians and priests are marked by a festive sense of delight, complete with ample wine and exuberant mariachi bands, reflecting a sheer joy in being invited to throw away their lives for Christ and his Church. As noted earlier, some bishops complain that the Legionaries "steal" funding and priestly vocations from their dioceses, and there may be something to that, although one may wonder whether they are not enlisting people and resources that would otherwise go unenlisted.

This pope has been very supportive of the Legionaries, as he has been supportive of many other renewal movements that are lighting the fires of devotion to the new evangelization. A journalist friend grumbles that this pope "has never met a right-wing group he doesn't like." But my friend's definition of "right-wing" is pretty close to being synonymous with anything this pope likes. He certainly likes Focolare, as did his predecessor and his predecessor before him. Focolare was founded in 1943 by Chiara Lubich in Italy. John XXIII approved the movement in 1962, and today it is active in Europe, North and South America, and Africa. Focolare includes celibate communities of men and women who follow the evangelical counsels of poverty, chastity, and obedience while carrying on their work in the world. There are also branches with married people, fraternities of priests, and a large youth organization.

Then there is the Neocatechumenal Way. They refer to themselves as the Way, while outsiders sometimes speak of the "Neocats." As the name suggests, here the focus is on deepening the catechesis of the Catholic people, giving them a solid foundation in the Church's doctrine and life. They are active in parishes, and some pastors have claimed they are divisive, giving the impression that anyone who is not part of the Way is a second-class Catholic. Many other bishops and priests report that their work has indeed engendered great parish renewal. While chiefly a lay movement, the Way also operates several seminaries which train priests for the dioceses where the seminaries are located. Newark, New Jersey, for example, has more than sixty priests associated with the Way. While at the synod I accept an invitation to lunch with several leaders of the Way. The ambiance and the food are superb, and the offering of testimonials of lives transformed by Christ is intensive. It is a little like a very Catholic version of my experience with some evangelical Protestants, and I am reminded of Paul VI's response to Clare Boothe Luce. She had all the zeal of a new convert, and it is reported that, as she was leaving a private audience with Paul VI, the pope was heard to say, "But Mrs. Luce, I already am a Catholic!"

Communion and Liberation (*Comunione e Liberazione*) had its beginnings in Italy in the 1950s when Father Luigi Giussani launched a youth movement that was at first associated with Catholic Action, but then became independent as Student Youth. During the student revolutions of 1968, many leaders of Student Youth embraced Marxist liberation movements, while others formed what came to be called

Communion and Liberation, the name indicating that authentic liberation of life comes through communion with Christ and his Church. The movement is loosely organized and there have been other submovements and splinters, but today Communion and Liberation claims one hundred thousand members in Italy and twenty thousand in other countries. The fraternity connected with the movement has been canonically recognized by Rome and has twenty-five thousand adult members who make a lifetime commitment, as well as a smaller number in Memores Domini ("Those Who Remember the Lord") who work in the world while observing the evangelical counsels. Communion and Liberation has gone through many transformations and has been variously involved in the seemingly infinite variousness of Italian politics, but the basic intention is still to be a youth movement. I am impressed by how many Italians in public life who are serious Catholics have their roots, one way or another, in *Comunione e Liberazione*. Several efforts to establish the movement in the United States have met with very limited success to date.

Then, of course, there is Opus Dei (Latin for "Work of God"), the renewal movement for which the word "controversial" might have been invented. Members refer simply to "the Work," and strongly prefer not to be called "Opies." I might as well confess that I have friends who are members of Opus Dei. (From the critics in the peanut gallery: "Ah ha! Just as we suspected!") I must also admit that I have never been able to see what they say they see in their basic text, *The Way*, a little book of 999 spiritual maxims written by the movement's founder, Josemaria Escriva de Balaguer, in the 1930s. But John Paul II obviously sees a lot that he likes in Opus Dei. Joachin Navarro-Valls, the very engaging press spokesman for the Holy See, is among the more prominent members of the Work. Recognized by Rome as a secular institute in 1947, Opus Dei was established by John Paul as a personal prelature in 1982, which means the members have as their bishop the prelate who heads the movement, Javier Echevarria Rodriguez, who is a papally appointed member of the synod. He makes a spirited intervention on, as you might expect, the vocation of the laity in the world.

The Work is emphatically a lay movement, with about eighty thousand members worldwide, and about two thousand priests for the pastoral care of its members. Some members of the Work may exaggerate the degree to which the movement anticipated Vatican II in "rediscovering" the vocation of the laity. As best I can determine, the very Spanish Catholicism of Monsignor Escriva was in the beginnings thoroughly preconciliar, but there is no doubt that the lay leadership that the movement cultivated during the Franco years was indispensable in Spain's peaceful transition to democracy. The movement today includes numeraries, who are celibate and live in centers maintained by the Way while working at various apostolates in the world; oblates, who embrace the celibate life but live outside the centers; and supernumeraries, who are married and have their own homes and careers. There are also cooperators, who support the movement while not being members. Opus Dei has major universities in Spain, Rome, and Latin America, as well as centers adjacent to many universities in the United States. At present they are building around the corner from where I live in New York City a large residence and U.S. headquarters, at 34th Street and Lexington Avenue.

These, then, are a few of the more conspicuous renewal movements, but there are many others. A member of the Roman Curia who follows such matters tells me that he estimates there are well over a million Catholic lay people involved in such movements, and millions more are influenced by them, but nobody knows for sure just how many since not all these insurgencies of lay devotion are canonically recognized by the Church. The larger movements maintain some kind of presence in Rome, and there I run into men and women associated with Latin American groups that I had never heard of, some of them claiming tens of thousands of members. And of course all of these are in addition to the hundreds of thousands of priests and laity in the long-established orders such as the Benedictines, Jesuits, Dominicans, and several varieties of Franciscans. These older movements of what the Church calls "the consecrated life" have been more or less taken for granted by Catholics. Since Vatican II many of them, especially in Europe and North America, seem to have lost a firm hold on their founding charism and have, as a consequence, experienced severe declines in both numbers and influence in the Church.

The Price, and the Hurt, of Discipleship

As has happened in earlier centuries, new movements arise to challenge what they view as the stultifying of the call to radical Christian

discipleship. Also as in earlier centuries, such movements stir controversy. Opus Dei in particular, but by no means alone, is the object of
regular attack in books and articles. There is a whole genre of literature generated by people who claim to have been connected with these
movements and then, for one reason or another, to have become bit-
terly disillusioned. Some of this literature is sober criticism, and some
of it is comparable to classic anti-Catholic polemics such as Maria
Monk's *Awful Disclosures of the Hotel Dieu Nunnery of Montreal*, first published in 1836 and still being reprinted today. There is no surprise in
the fact that some people have been hurt and disillusioned—in part
because movements that demand radical commitment attract also the
psychologically and spiritually unstable; in part because the failure to
meet the standards set by the community can be a grievous disap-
pointment; and in part because members and leaders of renewal movements, like all of us, are sinners and sometimes treat people shabbily.

Opus Dei and other groups are frequently accused of being, *inter
alia*, authoritarian, sexist, secretive, and elitist. Judged by the dominant
standards of a largely secularized culture, they are beyond reasonable
doubt guilty as charged. A society that cannot distinguish between
authoritarianism and the acknowledgment of what is authoritative is
scandalized by people who understand the whole of their lives in terms
of obedience to the lordship of Christ in accord with the rules of a
community of obedience. The recognition of difference and comple-
mentarity between male and female is likewise deeply offensive to prevailing cultural canons. And there is almost unavoidably a tone of
secretiveness that attends a powerful group identity, a sense of belonging to "us" as distinct from "them"—a sense greatly intensified by the
hostility of "them." As for elitism, what is the point of paying such a
steep price to belong to a group unless one believes it is the best?

All that being said, I am impressed that those whom I know in
these movements are, for the most part, keenly aware of the conventional criticisms and are eager to counter them. Against the charge of
authoritarianism, they accent the freedom of life lived in response to
commanding truth. Far from being sexist, they strive to demonstrate
mutual respect between men and women who know they are wondrously different. Against secretiveness, they enjoin upon members an
openness and invitational eagerness to share what they have found.
Against elitism, they espouse a humility that underscores the truth
that, whatever they have found and whatever they have achieved, it is

the grace of God from beginning to end. They seek, they strive, they enjoin, they espouse, and they often fail. It is a wonder that anybody should be surprised at that.

In some cases, there is the undeniable hurt felt by parents and families; in others, inexpressible gratitude that sons or daughters have found the purpose for which they were born. As a priest, I have encountered both reactions. For families, and especially for parents, there is a painful "letting go" of someone who has been claimed by a greater devotion, much as Mary proved her discipleship in releasing Jesus to his mission. In what are called the culture wars of our time, Christians frequently declare themselves to be "pro-family," but true Christianity sharply relativizes the natural bond of the family. The gospels are replete with the invitations of Jesus to leave all and follow him. "Truly, I say to you, there is no one who has left house or brothers or sisters or mother or father or children or lands, for my sake and for the gospel, who will not receive a hundredfold now in this time, houses and brothers and sisters and mothers and children and lands, with persecutions, and in the age to come eternal life" (Mark 10:29–30).

"With persecutions" is a nice touch. Through the centuries there has also been family resistance to those who respond to the call to radical discipleship. Francis of Assisi, Thomas Aquinas, Ignatius of Loyola, and innumerable others had to overcome the vigorous opposition of their families. Youthful passion is perceived as madness, and zeal for a vision of what might be possible is derided as fanaticism. Not for nothing are so many movements of renewal built around young people; not for nothing did Jesus say we must become as little children, or end up living and partly living lives that have displaced the possible with the practical. Movements that do not demand do not attract; movements that are incapable of scandalizing are incapable of renewing. They become, as Jesus said, salt that has lost its savor, good for nothing.

And I think again of Ratzinger's words in *Salt of the Earth*:

> In our time the reforms will definitely not come from forums and synods, though these have their legitimacy, sometimes even their necessity. Reforms will come from convincing personalities whom we may call saints. . . . If society in its totality is no longer a Christian environment, just as it was not in the first four or five centuries, the Church herself must form cells in which mutual support and a common journey, and thus the great vital milieu of the Church in miniature, can be experienced and put into practice.

An Awakening out of Control

At this Synod for America the repeated references to movements of renewal have to do with much more than the movements I have mentioned here, but they are crucially important to the renewal that is hoped for. Certainly that seems to be the understanding of John Paul II, who has so carefully nurtured these movements, protecting any flickering flame that may have been lighted by the Holy Spirit. The "new evangelization" may be something like a Great Awakening throughout the Americas, but its beginnings are elusive and under nobody's control. Certainly not under the control of this synod of bishops. It is the work of the Spirit, and the Spirit blows where He will. Also through, as Ratzinger says, "cells" that exemplify "the Church in miniature," and have the potential of igniting the Church in its magnitude. First the Church, then the world. "Go," said Ignatius to Francis Xavier, "and set the world on fire!"

Admittedly, the rhetoric of the synod is not so stirring, never mind inflammatory, as that. Here is a gathering of senior management, fretting over failed programs and dispiriting statistics, half-heartedly proposing fixes for what seems to be broken. But always—in tones sometimes wan and wistful, at other times urgent—there breaks out the insistence that it should not and need not be this way. Are not these senior managers also the successors of the apostles who once turned the world upside down? Are not portly prelates the same young men whose eyes once glistened with a vision of radical discipleship, of reckless self-abandonment in throwing their lives away for Christ, his Church, and his world? Of course they are the same men, however seasoned and sometimes jaded by experience, and evidence that most of them have not forgotten that long-ago vision keeps breaking through the incessant complaints about neoliberalism, external debt, vocational crises, demographic projections, and an unfriendly culture. Evidence breaks through at the mention of holiness. For times such as these, nothing less than holiness will do. As in a Great Awakening. As in an "Encounter with the Living Jesus Christ: The Way to Conversion, Communion, and Solidarity.

6

Freedom and the Script of History

Reevangelizing America with and Not against Those Who Differ

WHEN IN 1995 THE POPE issued the encyclical *Ut Unum Sint* ("That They Be One"), it seemed remote from the questions that have in recent decades preoccupied the Church in Latin America. In fact, many in Europe and North America also felt, at least at first, that the encyclical concerned them only indirectly. After all, it addressed the great subject of Christian unity primarily in terms of healing the breach between East and West. *Ut Unum Sint* reflected this pope's passionate hope for reconciliation between Rome and Orthodoxy so that, as he has often said, the Church might once again "breathe with both lungs." Although relations were frequently rocky over the centuries, the division between East and West is usually dated from 1054, when Rome and Constantinople formally excommunicated one another. There had been intermittent efforts at reconciliation since then, and a great step was taken when Paul VI and the ecumenical patriarch Athenagoras exchanged the kiss of peace in Rome and Constantinople, lifted the earlier excommunications, and recognized one another as "sister churches."

John Paul II fervently hoped that his pontificate would witness the completion of that healing. It now seems unlikely that that will happen on his watch, but he has laid the groundwork for its happening in the future, and he seems to believe it will happen sooner than many think. As the second millennium has been the millennium of Christian divisions, he says in *Ut Unum Sint*, so the third millennium must be the millennium of Christian unity. This pope has addressed the question of Christian unity, or ecumenism as it is called, more persistently and

117

extensively than any of his predecessors. In doing so, he has built upon and greatly strengthened the teaching of Vatican II's Decree on Ecumenism (*Unitatis Redintegratio*), and he has done so by unfolding the implications of the council's Dogmatic Constitution on the Church (*Lumen Gentium*). This may seem odd since *Lumen Gentium* is supposedly about how the Catholic Church understands itself, not about its relationship to other churches and communions.

It becomes increasingly evident, however, that those two questions cannot be separated. Precisely because the Catholic Church is what she claims to be, she finds herself inevitably entangled with other Christian communities. She is what she is only because of Christ, and Christ is not limited to the boundaries of the Catholic Church. As Johannes Cardinal Willebrands, then head of the Pontifical Council for Christian Unity, once put it, "Christ and the Church are coterminous." The Catholic Church presents itself as the Church most fully and rightly ordered through time, but that does not mean that it exhausts all that is meant by "the Church." *Ut Unum Sint* declares:

> It is not that beyond the boundaries of the Catholic community there is an ecclesial vacuum. Many elements of great value which in the Catholic Church are part of the fullness of the means of salvation and of the gifts of grace which make up the Church, are also found in the other Christian communities. . . . To the extent that these elements are found in other Christian communities, the one Church of Christ is effectively present in them. For this reason the Second Vatican Council speaks of a certain, though imperfect, communion.

The encyclical emphasizes that ecumenism is not an "appendix" or even a "program" of the Catholic Church but is inherent in the Catholic Church being what it claims to be. *Ut Unum Sint* also forges the strongest possible link between Christian unity and evangelization. The prayer of Jesus in John 17:21 that all his disciples may be one is a prayer that has evangelization in view—"so that the world may believe that thou hast sent me." It is not surprising, therefore, that a Synod for America that is focused on the "new evangelization" should give such prominent attention to ecumenism. Along with priestly vocations, the renewal of the laity, and economic conundrums, ecumenism became one of the big subjects of the synod. It was not always addressed under the rubric of ecumenism. More typically it came up in discussions of Protestant "sects" in Latin America, which are perceived as a particularly threatening component of the cultural imperialism of *El coloso del Norte*. Early on in the general sessions, the ecumenical issue arises, curiously enough, in connection with the Orthodox. I say curiously enough because Eastern Orthodoxy is not a numerically large phenomenon in North America and is even smaller in the South, although there are substantial Ukrainian and Melkite communities in Brazil and Argentina.

"The Journey Is Not Easy"

It happened this way. Shortly before the synod, the patriarch of Constantinople, Bartholomew, had visited the United States and in several public statements appeared to be retreating from the rapprochement with Rome. Bartholomew himself has had considerable ecumenical experience in the West and is viewed as a sympathetic figure, but he is under powerful pressure from Orthodox leaders who are wary of getting close to Rome. Some of them do not even recognize Catholics as fellow Christians, requiring the "rebaptism" of Catholics and other Christians who become Orthodox. With the end of Soviet Communism, Orthodoxy in places such as Russia is simultaneously in a state of revival and disarray. The ecumenical urgency of *Ut Unum Sint* may have inadvertently alarmed some Orthodox bishops and the influential monks of Mount Athos in Greece, who reacted with horror at the thought that the pope actually believes that full communion between East and West might be on the horizon. The patriarch of Moscow, Alexis II, has agreed to meetings with John Paul II and then reneged, reportedly at the insistence of his synod and of other bishops who thought the pace of reconciliation was much too fast, and who maybe wanted to stop it altogether.

Thus it was that, when Bartholomew came to the United States, he was perceived as being dangerously in advance of the churches that comprise the Orthodox Church. But at Georgetown University in Washington, D.C., and later in Baltimore, he delivered himself of views that startled his Catholic hosts. Far from affirming a course of inexorable reconciliation, he suggested at Georgetown that Orthodox and Catholics may in fact be growing farther apart and headed in quite different directions. Most dramatically, he proposed that between Catholic and Orthodox there is an "ontological difference" in the understanding of Christian faith and life. In the Baltimore meeting hosted by William Cardinal Keeler, Bartholomew observed that the ecumenical dialogue had not succeeded. The reason for this unhappy fact, he said, is not that there is a lack of love between the Orthodox and Catholics in dialogue, for there is love aplenty. The reason is to be found elsewhere. "It is by reason of an essential difference of how the mystery of the Church and salvation in her is realized," he said.

Ontological difference. Essential difference. And the difference is at the heart of what it means to be Christian—"the mystery of the Church and salvation." Cardinal Keeler very generously put the best construction on the words of Bartholomew in Washington and Baltimore, but Bartholomew's doleful analysis of ecumenical relations was the context for the synod intervention by Archbishop Stephen Sulyk of Philadelphia, who is metropolitan of Ukrainian Catholics in the United States. He shocked the assembly by flatly announcing that Bartholomew "has pronounced a sentence of death upon the ecumenical dialogue." We must now face the fact, he said, that the Orthodox reject us as heretics, just as we knew they did all along. The further fact is that "uniatism" has again been vindicated as the only "realistic" approach to relations between East and West.

Uniatism has a complicated history and in ecumenical circles is a pejorative term. It goes back to the Union of Brest in 1596 and denotes a process whereby Eastern churches enter into full communion with Rome but are allowed to retain their own liturgy and customs. Other Orthodox Christians tend to view the uniates as traitors and lackeys. In the judgment of those such as Archbishop Sulyk, however, the uniate churches are the appropriate "bridge" to the East. At the synod this is challenged by Archbishop Judson Michael Procyk of Pittsburgh, who is Ruthenian and bears the title of Metropolitan of the Byzantines. He strongly affirms the vision of *Ut Unum Sint* that looks to full reconciliation with the Orthodox churches. Outside the synod hall, Sulyk and Procyk conduct a lively reprise of an argument that has been going on for centuries. Briefly stated, the issue is whether the uniate churches are the way to reconciliation with the East or an obstacle to reconciliation. Sulyk takes the former position, while the ecumenical strategy of this pontificate has opted for the latter.

Cardinal Keeler, concerned that the questions raised by Bartholomew's visit might derail ecumenical advance, intervenes at the synod to praise the achievements of dialogue with the Orthodox, even as he acknowledges difficulties encountered. "These relations [with the Orthodox] were clouded when the collapse of communism opened the way to new freedom in Eastern and Central Europe. Our churches, with patience and mutual respect, now strive to move beyond these problems to return to the theological dialogue." He puts the best face on Bartholomew's statements in Baltimore, while he acknowledges that "this ecumenical journey is not an easy one." He notes that Edward Cardinal Cassidy will be leaving the synod for a few days to take a personal message from the Holy Father to the ecumenical patriarch on the day of St. Andrew, November 30. Andrew is the apostle to whom Constantinople appeals for its status as an ancient patriarchal see, along with Rome, Alexandria, Antioch, and Jerusalem.

Ecumenism Is Not Optional

Before he temporarily leaves the Synod, Cassidy makes a forceful intervention laying down an ecumenical marker for the synod's subsequent discussions. There are parallels, he suggests, between the Church in Latin America and the situation of the Orthodox in Eastern and Central Europe. In both cases, religious freedom has opened the way to new Christian groups that the older and more established churches see as threatening. In Russia, for instance, the Orthodox Church has vigorously promoted laws restricting the activities of other churches, including Catholics. Cassidy cautioned against such fearful reaction. There is no reason for the Catholic Church in Latin America to be so defensive, or to worry about an "invasion" of Protestants. Great care must be exercised in speaking of these groups as "sects." Certainly there can be no denial of the religious freedom of others, for such denial is "unworthy of the Catholic Church." Precisely where Catholics are in the majority they have the obligation to take the ecumenical initiative. Cassidy has been very supportive of the initiative in North America known as "Evangelicals and Catholics Together," and he suggests that the Church in the South might benefit by studying that effort. It would be, he says, "a great tragedy" for America were the

North and South divided in their commitment to Christian unity, "as though ecumenism was a mandate only for some and not for all."

The gist of the cardinal's message is unmistakable. The insurgency of Protestants in Latin America creates problems, but also opportunities. Catholics must not return hostility with hostility. Above all, respect for other Christians and determined efforts to cultivate our unity in Christ are not optional for Catholics. They are an inherent and undeniable mandate that is inseparable from the Catholic Church's understanding of itself. I expect there are some synod fathers who respond to Cassidy's intervention somewhat dismissively. After all, they might think, he is just doing his job as the member of the Curia in charge of ecumenism; he is merely saying what you would expect someone in his position to say. But informal conversations suggest that most recognize that Cassidy's intervention, offered early on in the proceedings, is both a warning and an invitation that is not to be ignored.

The Church's teaching notwithstanding, many Latin American bishops feel themselves sorely provoked by evangelical and pentecostal "invaders." During the course of the synod, I am told numerous horror stories about Protestants setting up loudspeakers around Catholic churches in order to disrupt services, about families and whole villages divided by campaigns of anti-Catholic propaganda, about television and radio preachers who declare the Church to be the Antichrist and publicly mock the Blessed Virgin. One cannot help but sympathize, understanding why talk about ecumenism may seem like an unrealistic counsel of sweetness and light in circumstances of great ugliness. In his long keynote address at the beginning of the synod, Cardinal Sandoval of Mexico spoke of a "veritable invasion of sects" in Central America, the Caribbean, and South America. The invasion is "so extensive as to represent a coordinated plan to change the present religious identity of Latin America," he declared. Much later in the synod, after all the interventions touching on ecumenism, there are still broadside attacks on "the sects" in the reports issuing from the small groups. It is all part of a vast conspiracy led by the United States. The report from one Spanish group speaks of "an organized campaign financed to destroy the Catholic Church because of its criticism of neoliberalism."

Archbishop Oscar Lipscomb of Mobile, Alabama, intervenes to say that religious pluralism, long a fact of life in North America, is increasingly the reality also in the South. I am reminded of the observation of

Father John Courtney Murray, a Jesuit who played a critical role in the Church's developing doctrine on religious freedom, that it seems God has allowed pluralism to be written into the script of history. Pluralism may seem threatening, Lipscomb notes, and can generate "reaction, recrimination, and appeals for repression," but such a response fosters only "greater separation and ever-deeper misunderstanding." The archbishop's theme is "ecumenism in service to evangelization," which is precisely the linkage of mandates encouraged by *Ut Unum Sint*—the mandate to be one and the mandate to evangelize. Each mandate is in the service of the other.

As a bishop in the American South, Lipscomb says he experienced in the struggle against segregation under the leadership of Martin Luther King, Jr., the mutual strengthening that ecumenism can provide. Similarly, he believes Catholics and Protestants deepened the level of trust between them as they worked together for human rights in Central America during the turbulent 1980s. Of course Catholics are a small minority in Alabama, and the experiences to which he alludes are mainly with black and liberal oldline churches which are worlds removed from the phenomenon of the "sects" in Latin America. Nonetheless, his way of making the connections between ecumenism and evangelization can, he hopes, move the discussion forward. The archbishop's words carry some weight on these questions, since he has not only headed up the U.S. bishops' conference's committee on ecumenism, but he has also taken over from the late Joseph Cardinal Bernardin of Chicago the leadership of "Common Ground," a project aimed at alleviating tensions within the Church in the United States between liberals and conservatives, traditionalists and progressives, as the various parties are commonly called. Working on intra-Catholic conflicts is not exactly ecumenism and may seem unrelated to evangelization, but it is an effort to prevent, as the archbishop says, "greater separation and ever-deeper misunderstanding."

A "Controversial" Intervention

I was grateful that Cardinal Schotte called for my intervention at the very best time, right before the morning coffee break. Speak at the beginning of the session and what you say is buried under dozens of

subsequent speeches, while at the end of the session people are wearied by listening and eager to get away for *pranzo* and whatever the afternoon holds. The coffee break is the only time during general sessions where there is general discussion of what has been said in the aula. I began by stating my theme, "evangelicals and Catholics together." The Holy Father, I noted, has invited us to prepare for the third millennium as a "springtime" of world evangelization and of Christian unity. How to bring together the imperative to evangelize and the imperative to Christian unity? If we can answer that, the prospect is breathtaking: "In the next century, evangelical Protestants and Roman Catholics can evangelize and re-evangelize *with* one another rather than against one another."

There are about two billion Christians in the world, I observed, about one third of the world's population. One billion are Catholic and "the other large, vibrant, and rapidly growing sector of the Christian movement in world history is evangelical Protestantism, including most of those known as pentecostals." When we say "the evangelicals" we mean those Protestants, such as Baptists and Assemblies of God, who for various reasons have not been part of the ecumenical movement of this century. "Unlike the so-called historic Protestant communities with whom we have been in formal dialogue for a long time," I said, "the evangelicals tend to be suspicious of ecumenism and are often strongly anti-Catholic."

As for their frequent hostility to us, I thought it best to bite the bullet this way: "They often do not view us as brothers and sisters in Christ, but we are obliged to view them as brothers and sisters in Christ. According to the teaching of *Lumen Gentium*, they are those who are baptized and believe in Christ and are therefore 'truly but imperfectly in communion' with the Catholic Church. Recognizing that communion, we should permanently eliminate all reference to 'sects' when speaking of those who are in fact brothers and sisters in Christ. We are their brothers and sisters, whether or not they want to be our brothers and sisters. The rich ecclesiology of *Lumen Gentium* is both our blessing and burden. It is the blessing of God's revealed truth, and it is the burden of our responsibility to reach out to the evangelicals, even when they do not reach out to us."

I referred to the work of "Evangelicals and Catholics Together" over the past five years, how so many evangelicals and Catholics had

discovered one another in the pro-life movement and other cultural tasks, and how these encounters had led to serious theological conversations which, with the invaluable help of the Pontifical Council for Christian Unity, have produced a common statement on the doctrine of justification by grace through faith, "The Gift of Salvation." I noted that the driving force of evangelical missionary activity among Catholics—commonly condemned as proselytizing or sheep stealing—is their belief that Catholics do not teach justification by grace through faith. To the extent it meets with agreement, "The Gift of Salvation" puts that question to rest. At the same time, I suggested, we must ask ourselves why so many people claim to have encountered the living Jesus Christ under evangelical auspices in a way they had not known as Catholics.

I mentioned the meeting in New York, just a month before the synod, of evangelical leaders and Latin American bishops brought together by CELAM. "Already," I said, "some evangelical leaders recognize that in predominantly Catholic cultures the cause of the gospel must be advanced in cooperation with the Catholic Church. This is a monumental change and it is only beginning to get underway. Only God knows where it will lead, but we must carefully nurture these beginnings." I concluded with an attempt at rhetorical flourish: "In his inaugural homily in October, 1978, the Holy Father exhorted us, 'Be not afraid!' My esteemed fathers, brothers, and sisters, let this synod clearly say that, as we cross the threshold of the third millennium, we are not afraid to act on the bold but not impossible vision of 'evangelicals and Catholics together.' May Our Lady of Guadalupe assist us on this way of ecumenical and evangelistic courage."

Reactions were not slow in coming, including a smile and wave from the Holy Father which I chose to interpret as encouragement. As the synod fathers were leaving the aula, many offered congratulations, and I was struck that several described the intervention as "prophetic." In church circles, "prophetic" has a touch of ambiguity about it. It can be a compliment meaning bold and farsighted. As often as not, it can mean far out and impossibly unrealistic. As subsequent discussions would make clear, both meanings were undoubtedly in play. Several days later, a curial cardinal told me that mine was the most "controversial" intervention to date. I don't think he meant it as a compliment. On the other hand, an American archbishop with extensive ecumenical experience tells me that he had been trying in vain to make the same point to the Latin American bishops for thirty years and for the first time he thought it got through.

A Time for Realism

Panama's Lacunza Maestrojuan has had extensive ecumenical experience and was one of the bishops at the New York meeting with evangelicals. He underscores how offended other Christians are by our use of the term "sects," and urges that it simply be excised from our Catholic vocabulary when in fact we are referring to fellow Christians. He is a large and imposing figure, with an impressive shock of prematurely white hair, and there is a hint of impatience in his tone. He has too often run into the view that Christian unity is something of an optional question for people who are interested in "that sort of thing," and he is pleased to see it receiving such major attention here. Not by everyone, however. In both small groups and general sessions, the view is expressed that "the problem of the sects" is exaggerated, that in most countries of Latin America they are making little headway. One bishop invokes a "study" that presumably shows that Catholics who join up with the evangelical groups generally return within two or three years. "They know where the Church is," he concludes smilingly. Or perhaps the word is smugly.

Antonio Moreno Casamitjana, archbishop of Concepcion, Chile, strikes a very different note. It is time for a sober and humble realism, he says. Far from being a marginal phenomenon, the evangelical and pentecostal movements now claim more than 30 percent of once-Catholic Chile. "We must ask why, and that means we must examine our conscience." He provides a catalogue of Catholic failures, including a lack of clergy, poor formation of clergy, pastoral aloofness and rigidity, and, perhaps most important, the failure to thoroughly catechize the faithful in the Bible and church teaching. To be sure, he adds, it is not simply that the Church has failed. "The political and cultural dynamics of recent years have often been hostile to the Church, and the new Christian movements are often aggressive and unfair in their tactics." But it is not helpful to put all the blame on others. It is true that they have the dollars and the more sophisticated use of the media, "but there are too many people who say that they did not 'find God' in the Church because we have been too preoccupied with the horizontal dimensions of Christian faith and life." He concludes with a call for a robustly confident "new evangelization" that accents what is distinctive about Catholicism and unabashedly puts the encounter with the transcendent reality of God at the center of Christian experience.

There is a basic difference in our Catholic situation, and it is both a strength and a weakness, suggests Gordon Anthony Pantin, archbishop of Port of Spain, Trinidad. "The newer Protestant movements are united in their anti-Catholicism. We try to reach out to them and maybe some day we will have the success that Father Neuhaus speaks about, but it is very difficult." One difficulty, he suggests, is that Catholic teaching requires us to recognize elements of truth not only in other Christian groups but also in other religions. For instance, he believes he has the support of St. Paul in allowing Catholics to take part in Hindu festivals, as long as they do not eat meat sacrificed to idols or otherwise compromise their Christian faith.

Archbishop Pantin here touches on a cluster of questions that preoccupy sociologists of religion. Movements that are sectarian in the sociological sense of the term propose an unequivocal choice of either/or, and making that choice provides a powerful measure of cohesiveness. Catholicism, by contrast, is culturally affirmative and embracing, always seeking out what can legitimately be taken in. That is what is meant by the much-discussed concept of "inculturation." That is part of what James Joyce meant in saying that Catholicism is Here Comes Everybody. As the archbishop notes, that makes it hard to engage sympathetically the either/or of evangelical Protestantism, and doubly hard when their either/or is posed against the Catholic Church.

What makes Catholicism different is also what makes it strong, suggests Bishop Jose Maria Arancedo of Argentina. We need prophets, he says, who call us back to the excitement and distinctiveness of our calling. Bishops are not politicians or technicians, he says, in what I take to be an implicit criticism of excessive preoccupation with fixing political and economic systems. Moreover, the Catholic Church preaches not only the salvation of isolated individuals but "holds forth a hopeful vision of the unity of mankind." Catholicism is comprehensively *catholic* in a way that other presentations of Christianity are not. Only the Catholic Church, he says, is in a position "to call mankind to a planetary vigil of the third millennium." Arancedo's intervention has echoes of John Paul II's "Be not afraid!" in proposing a coherent, comprehensive, and compelling vision of the human future.

Different Ways of Being Christian

The archbishop of Caracas, Venezuela, is Ignacio Velasco Garcia, and he takes a distinct tack on the evangelical challenge. Catholics, he suggests, should not have to be taught by others the meaning of "the gift of salvation." That salvation is a gift and that it is received by faith, which is also a gift, has always been the teaching of the Catholic Church. The implication is that it is our fault if that has not been understood, either by Catholics or by others. He is open to a number of proposed responses to the challenge of other Christians, but the first and most important response is, "Preach the Catholic faith!"

We heard earlier the impressive reflection of Alfonso Cabezas Aristizabal of Colombia on the importance of popular piety. All this talk about "the sects," he says, reflects a fearfulness that the opponents of the Church readily exploit. The answer to fear is to recognize that the Spirit of God is moving mightily among the Catholic people in small groups of prayer and study, in charismatic renewal, in apparitions and other signs and wonders. "Catholicism affirms a theology of creation in which God works through water, salt, light, and the devotion of ordinary people." The bishop's insight, as impressive as it is, can easily be turned in another and more questionable direction. That direction is to respond to the evangelical challenge by simply dividing up the religious market. This assumes that there is a distinctly Catholic way of being Christian and a distinctly Protestant way of being Christian, and contending parties should find the piece of the market that fits their product. Niche marketing, as economists call it, is not evangelization. Yet in the synod discussions, as also in the preparatory documents, there are a few troubling suggestions that Catholics should simply stick with what they're good at and what the "opposition" completely lacks—Marian devotions, pilgrimages, the cult of the saints, miracles, water, salt, and light.

It may be that the full panoply of Catholic devotional excitements will be more attractive to more people than the intense "born again" experience and moral rigorism of evangelical insurgency, but to put the question this way is to be engaged in marketing rather than evangelization. The marketing of the gospel—replete with statistics, flow charts, growth strategies, and self-promoting ballyhoo of almost every imaginable kind—is one of the more unseemly aspects of much of evangelical Protestantism. It would be a pity were Catholics to try to imitate it. In addition to which, we would probably not be very good at it. The greater pity would be in betraying the ecumenical imperative to engage brothers and sisters in Christ by treating them simply as the competition in the religious marketplace. This would be unbridled capitalism—or "neoliberalism," as some would have it—carried to the nth degree. But the greatest of pities would be to refuse the challenge of entering with others into a fuller understanding of the gospel as "the gift of salvation" which God intends for all Christians to propose to all people.

In fact, some synod fathers say, we have a great deal to learn from these other Christians. Roberto Gonzalez of Corpus Christi, Texas, is a younger bishop who appeals to the very old biblical idea of "stewardship" and its potential for renewal both within the Church and in relating to others—or, as he puts it, *ad intram et ad extram*. He speaks under the rather unpromising title of "Stewardship: Concretizing the Implications of Solidarity." But what he has to say is fresher than the title suggests. Stewardship applies to the connection between the churches in the North and those in the South, says the bishop, quoting St. Paul in 2 Corinthians 8:13–14: "I do not mean that others should be eased and you burdened, but that as a matter of equality your abundance at the present time should supply their wants, that there may be equality." The experience of the evangelicals can teach us, Gonzalez suggests. Countering the assertion that Protestant growth is an invasion bankrolled by the North, he lifts up the way in which evangelicals have successfully encouraged practices of stewardship and tithing—*mayordomia cristiana*, as they call it—that not only support their programs but also deepen their commitment to Christ.

Perhaps we do not ask enough of our own people. Especially when they are poor, we view them as victims, as people incapable of being the artisans of their own destiny, incapable of being active subjects in the great enterprise of the gospel. That was a note struck by Father John Corriveau, general of the Capuchin friars, who has long pastoral experience in Latin America. Part of the success of the Protestant movements, he urged, is that they expect great things of their people, they think them capable of great things, and as a result lay people have a powerful sense of responsibility for evangelization, and for all other aspects of their community's life. His intervention and others make the point, no doubt uncomfortable to some, that self-examination cannot help but induce a humility that is ready to learn from others, even when those others are anything but friendly.

That is taken up by Archbishop (soon to be Cardinal) Dario Castrillon Hoyos, a Colombian who is pro-prefect of the Congregation for the Clergy. He agrees that it is no longer tolerable to dismiss as "sects" those who are in fact brothers and sisters in Christ. He speaks frankly: "The traditional culture, especially in Latin America, finds it difficult to accept ecumenical attitudes. We ought to change our thinking about ecumenism. We should learn how to maintain our identity while being open to the theological and moral values of other creeds, despite the fact that some of these other religious movements reject or insult the Catholic Church." Such change comes hesitantly, in stops and spurts, and frequent missteps. Also among those who have the best of will, such as Archbishop Hoyos, it can happen that the change in thinking about ecumenism falls short of recognizing that ecumenism is not about "other creeds" and "religious movements" but about the one movement that shares the one creed, however variously expressed, that Jesus Christ is Lord.

Ecumenisms True and False

In my intervention I spoke of the Catholic Church's self-understanding as set forth in *Lumen Gentium*, and how it is that non-Catholic Christians are in "true but imperfect" communion with the Church. A Colombian bishop remarks to me, "Perhaps, Father, Latin America is not ready for *Lumen Gentium*." He said it with a smile, of course, but there may be more than a little truth in his wry observation. And it applies not only to Latin America. In the United States there is not the same intense conflict between Protestant and Catholic, but that is not, or at least not chiefly, because Catholics have internalized the teaching of *Lumen Gentium*, never mind the comprehensive ecumenical vision of *Ut Unum Sint*. What is called "ecumenism" in North America is often driven by a social and historical circumstance commonly described as "pluralism." Theological reflection, such as the ecclesiology of *Lumen Gentium*, comes along after the fact. It provides a rationale for the "live and let live" attitude that is made necessary by the fact of religious pluralism. Some Catholic critics of pluralism condemn this attitude as "indifferentism," by which they mean that people are indifferent to the differences, especially the doctrinal differences, that should make the most difference. Ecumenism, they charge, is the triumph of social harmony over religious truth.

That criticism should not be dismissed lightly. Ecumenism is easily confused with mere tolerance. To be sure, there is nothing "mere" about tolerance in situations where the alternative is violent intolerance. In such situations, tolerance is a civic virtue to be highly prized. But tolerance falls far short of the ecumenical moment that is a shared encounter with the truth that compels us to recognize one another as brothers and sisters in Christ. For example, an encounter such as "Evangelicals and Catholics Together" must be wholly in service to God's truth or else it lacks moral and intellectual integrity. At the same time, that does not prevent us from recognizing that such an encounter in truth and for truth is made possible, in large part, by the social and historical experience of pluralism. Such pluralism has not been the experience of most of Latin America.

From the first evangelization by the Spanish and Portuguese more than five hundred years ago, the Church in Latin America has had an ambivalent relationship to political power. One must be careful not to generalize too broadly, for Latin America is large and various. And it is true that orders such as the Franciscans, Dominicans, and Jesuits attempted to chart alternative patterns of evangelization here and there. But the pattern of Catholicism was generally one of alliance with state authority. What it means to be a "Catholic country" or a "Catholic culture" was not limited to the assumption that the over-

whelming majority of people, in some cases almost all the people, are
Catholic. That assumption was formally countenanced, and in many
cases explicitly stated, in the constitutional self-understanding of
nations. This gave the appearance of a Catholic Church with immense
power but, as the bishops meetings since Medellin have come to recognize ever more clearly, such power was, more often than not, illu-
sory. Tacit and official alliances with the state frequently resulted in
the captivity of the Church to the established order.

The liberation theology that gained such influence in the 1970s
and 1980s was, in many respects, a protest against that captivity to the
established order of politics, economics, and culture. It aimed at a revolutionary overturning of the old order of what was viewed as an
oppressive "Christendom," but, ironically, it proposed replacing the
old order with a new and revolutionary version of Christendom. This
irony should not surprise us. In the course of the Church's history
throughout the world, it has often been the case that the hoped-for cor-
rection of one problem has resulted in the problem's reappearance in
a different and even more troubling form. But it is true of the life of
the Church, as it is true in the life of individuals, that, in the words of
Charles Peguy, "God writes straight with crooked lines." The agitations
of liberation theology, now separated from its Marxist ideology, can be
seen as a necessary phase in the Church's discovery of its distinctive
role in the social order. Nor should it be surprising that the discovery
of that role is being forced, in large part, by the aggressive presence of
Christian movements challenging the Catholic hegemony.

The Permanence and Promise of Pluralism

The traditional Catholic monopoly assumed a social circumstance that
is the opposite of pluralism. The opposite of pluralism is monism,
which means an intact, cohesive social order in which there is a unity,
or at least a synchronization, of political, economic, and cultural
authority. In such a monistic order, the idea of a Catholic state in a
Catholic society not only makes sense but is probably necessary. A certain school of Catholic social teaching prior to the Second Vatican
Council viewed this arrangement as the "thesis" that the Church must

support. The same school viewed a pluralistic social order as the "hypothesis" that the Church could tolerate provisionally until it was in a position to establish the "thesis." Prior to the council, Catholic thinkers in North America debated this question with reference to the "thesis" of Franco Spain and the "hypothesis" of the United States. I have mentioned Father John Courtney Murray's observation that "pluralism is written into the script of history." That is to say, pluralism is not a circumstance that the Church should strive to overcome by the political and legal establishment of its own hegemony but is the permanent condition of a free Church in a free society.

This understanding of the Church's posture in society meets with strong opposition, not least of all in Latin America, because it is viewed as an imposition of a U.S. model on the rest of the world. There is no disputing the fact that there are problems with the American model. For instance, "the separation of church and state" can lead to the separation of religion from public life, a circumstance in which religion is thoroughly marginalized and confined to the so-called private sphere of life. In America that is the dismal doctrine frequently imposed by the courts in their reading (i.e., misreading) of the Religion Clause of the First Amendment. At the same time, however, the actual social fact in the United States is one of vibrant religious communities and of religiously grounded morality in vigorous, although typically confused, interaction with the public culture. Writing in the 1830s, Alexis de Tocqueville observed that religion is "the first political institution of American democracy." By that he meant that it was in the voluntary associations of religion that Americans learned the habits and guiding moral truths of political participation. What was true in the 1830s is, *mutatis mutandis*, true today.

Does this mean that Latin America should accept, or even must accept, the U.S. model of religious pluralism? The answer, needless to say, is complex. The countries of Latin America will have to develop their own ways of responding to the challenge of pluralism, but the challenge will not go away. The several Protestant insurgencies in Latin America are one part of the challenge. In fact they touch on the most critical part of the challenge, which is cultural. That observation assumes the priority of culture over politics and economics. This is not to say that politics and economics are unimportant, but simply that politics is, in largest part, a function of culture. Culture provides the traditions, mores, ideas, and aspirations by which people understand themselves. At the heart of culture is religion, which means the commanding truths by which people try to make sense of their lives. At the heart of culture, both linguistically and sociologically, is *cult*. Culture reflects what a people revere and, finally, what they worship.

Politics, on the other hand, is succinctly defined by Aristotle as "Free persons deliberating the question, How ought we to order our life together?" The "ought" in that question clearly indicates that politics is, above all, a moral enterprise. Not, of course, a moral enterprise in the sense that politicians are necessarily moral, but a moral enterprise in the sense that the activity of asking what *ought* to be done—what is fair? what is just? what serves the common good?—is moral in nature. In a free society, the question of how we ought to order our life together is answered by reference to the traditions, mores, ideas, aspirations, and commanding truths that make up the culture. It is in this sense that politics is, in largest part, a function of culture.

Cultural Identity Protected and Engaged

Culture. Politics. Economics. In Latin American eyes, the Protestant insurgency is frequently seen primarily as a facet of economic imperialism extending its tentacles from the North. The economic juggernaut directed from the United States appears to be both alien and unstoppable. It carries with it its own political and cultural dynamics, and one can understand why some view "the sects" as the religio-cultural agent of American imperialism. In the jargon of the social sciences, the United States is the world's "lead society." The world deserves a much worthier lead society, but for the present and for the foreseeable future there is no other candidate to challenge the American hegemony. This must not be seen, however, only in terms of an American imposition. Imposition works hand in hand with attraction. The influence of the United States—culturally, politically, economically—cannot be explained apart from the attractiveness of what the United States offers and is seen to represent. The undeniable fact is that most of the people of the world, including the people of Latin America, want what they perceive Americans to have. This is obviously true of consumer goods, but also of movies, music, fashions—and, yes, the deeper dimension of culture that is religion. One may well argue that people should *not* want what they perceive Americans to have, but it is usually a thankless task to argue people out of their desires.

In *Tongues of Fire: The Explosion of Protestantism in Latin America*, the British sociologist David Martin writes incisively about "the Americanization of Latin American religion." The Latin American bishops at the synod, and no doubt most thoughtful Catholics, resist that prospect. The instinct of resistance is, I believe, right. In any event, given the long history of resentment against the impositions of the North, such resistance is almost inevitable. Such resistance need not be blind or undiscriminating, however. There are aspects of the "invasion" from the North that are probably inevitable, some of which should be welcomed. It would seem that the expansion of the market economy—whether called "neoliberalism" or "globalization"—cannot be stopped except by countries that adopt statist or socialist measures that end up by excluding the great majority of their own people from what *Centesimus Annus* calls "the circle of productivity and exchange." It is very doubtful that many countries, especially if they are democratic and free, can muster the political will to impose such measures or sustain them over time. That is simply because, for better *and* for worse, people want what the market provides.

Both Marxists and the champions of laissez-faire capitalism (in North America, the latter are called libertarians) subscribe to the doctrine of the priority of the economic. The Synod for America makes it clear that there are bishops who subscribe to that doctrine as well. In the Marxist and libertarian view, economics is the "base" and culture is the "superstructure," economics is the "phenomenon" and culture the "epiphenomenon." Among the problems with attributing priority to the economic is that it consigns the Church to being perpetually epiphenomenal. The business of the Church, if one may speak of the Church having a business, is culture. That is to say, the Church provides a "meaning system" by which people understand, in the light of eternity, who they are and how they are to live. In the current jargon, this is their "identity." In the modern world, everybody walks around with what sociologist Peter Berger calls an "identity kit."

It is a kit of many parts, including family, friends, sex, skills, region, class, occupation, nation, and much else. In unpacking our identity kit, we tell people who we are. The Christian proposal is that we are—above all else and fulfilling all else—members of Christ and his Church. The work of "inculturation" is to integrate, as best we can, that overriding identity with all the other items in our identity kits. Identity becomes a problem in the modern world—it becomes even an "identity crisis"—because who we are is increasingly not something given but something chosen. Identity is less and less a matter of ascription, of being assigned a certain identity by virtue of, for example, our parentage or place of birth. Rather, identity is a matter of election; given a daunting and growing range of possibilities, we *decide* who we are. The disturbing, but also liberating, consequence is that less and less can be taken for granted, more and more is up for grabs.

Facing Up to Modernity

The result is the notorious differentiation and fragmentation of society. This can be disorienting, and it is little wonder that many long for an intact world that wards off the disorientation by providing a firm and more or less unchallengeable definition of who we are and how we are to live, as in an intact "Catholic culture" where one is Catholic by osmosis rather than by decision. Recognizing the priority of culture and that at the heart of culture is cult, we come to understand that the religious implication of modernity is voluntarism. At a very deep level— at a level deeper than habit and sensibilities formed by tradition—religious voluntarism grates against the Catholic way of being Christian. Religious voluntarism, it is commonly thought, is the distinctively Protestant way of being Christian. The Catholic way of being Christian accents the community rather than the individual. In the Catholic way, the Church is not a voluntary association formed by like-minded individuals but the Body of Christ into which we are sacramentally incorporated. For the Catholic, being Christian is not a matter of our choosing but of our being chosen.

The Catholic way of being Christian is different not just in ideas, doctrines, or church organization; it is different in its very "feel" and "touch." It is living life in sacramental *communio* with Christ and his Church, with the saints past and present, in a life-defining posture of faith's obedient echo of Mary's *fiat*—"Let it be to me according to your word." For the Catholic, there is an experience of cultural dissonance, if not "culture shock," in the encounter with Protestantism—especially with Protestantism in its evangelical, pentecostal, and revivalistic versions. The stress that these Protestants place on individual decision and religious experience, combined with their strict moralism and insistence on an exclusive evangelistic language of "winning souls for Christ," seem threatening to the Catholic way of being Christian.

We have heard interventions at the synod suggesting that Catholics in North America, because of the pluralistic and dominantly Protestant circumstance in which they live, are more Protestant than they suspect. This may be viewed either as an achievement or as a failure. As an achievement, it can be described as the successful "inculturation" of Catholicism in the North American context. As a failure, it can be described as an uncritical accommodation and loss of Catholic identity. In fact—and as is usually the case in the real world—it is a mixed bag, a confused amalgam of achievement and failure. Certainly the Church in North America is in no position to recommend the adoption of its experience as the model for the future of Latin America. And yet Latin America is increasingly faced with the challenge of the same modernizing dynamics that are so familiar in the North. These dynamics are not going to go away. They are almost certain to become more intense. We must therefore hope that the Church in Latin America will deal with them more successfully than has the Church in the North.

In speaking of modernizing dynamics, we do not overlook the fact that large parts of Latin America are very modern indeed, and have been for a long time. North Americans are inclined to view the South as "underdeveloped" or "third world," but at least the urbanized elite sectors of countries such as Argentina, Brazil, and Chile are undoubtedly participants in what is called the modern world. That is true technologically and economically, and, with the continuing growth of democracy in their recent history, also politically. But it is only ambiguously the case with respect to culture. The hope of many Latin American thinkers is that the "modernity project" is not a package that is all of a piece. Those who embrace that hope want to buy into the technological, economic, and political advantages of modernity while maintaining an intact culture, which in most cases means a Catholic culture. Against that hope are the arguments of those who say that modernity is a "brutal bargain," an all-or-nothing proposition.

The question, then, is whether the economic, political, and cultural are a package, or whether they are more like a Tinkertoy set, in which the pieces can be taken apart, allowing societies to accept some features of modernity and reject others. The Protestant insurgency, which brings with it religious voluntarism and cultural pluralism, is the part of the modernity project that many Catholics want to reject. I think it likely, however, that it cannot be separated from the package. Earlier in this century, Max Weber famously argued for a powerful connection between capitalism and what he called the Protestant ethic. Individual decision, initiative, innovation, and entrepreneurship, he contended, are uniquely cultivated by sensibilities attached to the Protestant way of being Christian. Weber's argument has been much debated over the years, and some scholars, notably Michael Novak, have done pioneering work in making the case that "the spirit of democratic capitalism" is thoroughly compatible with—indeed more securely grounded in—Catholic Christianity. The frontal challenge to the claims of Weber and his acolytes is made explicit in the title of Novak's *The Catholic Ethic and the Spirit of Democratic Capitalism*.

The Difference Is Indigenous

These are arguments of crucial importance to the future of the Church in Latin America, and indeed in all the Americas. Whether or not Latin Americans are persuaded by such arguments, the cultural challenge at its deepest level, which is religious, cannot be wished away. It is very difficult, if not impossible, to envision a future for an intact, monistic, monopolistic "Catholic culture." First, the Protestant insurgency is deeply entrenched and rapidly growing. Admittedly, the growth is frequently exaggerated. Evangelical Protestants are much inclined to hyperbole, and one encounters incredible claims about their "winning" this country or that country for Christ (which means winning it for Protestantism) within the next five years, or ten years, or whatever schedule is set. Such claims are to be generally discounted, although the Protestant advance in places as diverse as Guatemala and

Chile are impressive indeed. But whether the reality is a Protestant "explosion," as David Martin would have it, or a matter of incremental growth, evangelical Protestantism is a permanent phenomenon in Latin America.

Moreover, it is mainly an *indigenous* phenomenon. At the synod, this seemed the hardest truth for many bishops to accept. "For every one dollar we have for evangelization," declared one bishop concerned about the foreign invasion, "the sects get a hundred dollars from the North." This is a dangerous misperception. Even were it true, how could anyone cut off the flow of evangelical resources from the North? One Latin American bishop tells me, "This is something that the Church in your country has to deal with." The U.S. episcopal conference should tell the Southern Baptist Convention that they can no longer support missions in Latin America? The American bishops cannot do that and, were they to try, it would make no difference. More pertinently, it should not be done because it would violate both American principle and, more important, the Church's teaching about religious freedom. Is the growth of evangelical movements in Latin America significantly aided by real or perceived support from the North? That is no doubt the case. For many Latin Americans, Protestantism is attractive because it is seen as a component of the "American way of life" that they desire. For many others, it is unattractive because it is part of a cultural invasion that they fear. But the crucial fact is that evangelical Protestantism has become a predominantly indigenous movement within Latin America. Were every dollar, every evangelistic crusade, and every piece of communications technology from the North to be cut off tomorrow—which is not going to happen— the Catholic Church in Latin America would be facing essentially the same challenge from "the sects."

A number of synodical interventions frankly acknowledged that a great strength of the evangelical insurgency is that it provides people with an intensity of religious experience they had not known as Catholics. Of course, a good many people move back and forth between the Church, on the one hand, and Protestant groups, on the other, all the while considering themselves perfectly good Catholics. Thus, even one person can encompass what might be called a kind of religious pluralism. This is hardly new in Latin America. In Cuba, for instance, many Catholics have long practiced Santeria, and in countries such as Brazil there is a veritable carnival of syncretistic cults that coexist in jumbled confusion with Catholicism. These are confusions that have long since been inculturated, so to speak, by Catholicism. The new thing with the evangelical movements is that they shatter that comfortable coexistence by calling for a decision one way or the other.

The decision is usually called a "decision for Christ," and it is typically accompanied by a decision against the Catholic Church. But it is the power of that decision for Christ that many bishops recognize is all too often missing from the Catholic experience. The very theme of the synod—"Encounter with the Living Jesus Christ: The Way to Conversion, Communion, and Solidarity"—has a definitely Protestant ring to it, one bishop tells me. Another suggests that the evangelicals have much to say about "encounter" and about "conversion," but Catholics are the experts on "communion and solidarity." That seems to be a questionable way of putting the matter. Certainly it must be asked why so many Catholics do not have a converting, life-transforming, encounter with the living Jesus Christ. Among Catholics in the charismatic and *cursillo* movements, of course, such dramatic spiritual encounters are much encouraged and, as a consequence, become almost commonplace. But the Catholic strategy cannot be limited to competing in the religious marketplace by offering comparable, or even more intense, religious experiences.

Self-Reliance and a Different Women's Movement

We must question the claim that Catholics have some kind of monopoly on "communion and solidarity." To be sure, evangelicals cannot provide *communio* in all its ecclesial and sacramental richness, and often do not promote solidarity along the lines of the Church's social teaching about, for instance, the preferential option of the poor. Yet it is a grave mistake to think that the Protestant insurgency does not offer communion and solidarity, at least as those terms are defined sociologically. Quite the opposite is the case. All the studies of these movements emphasize the importance of small communities of mutual support. Such support is not only spiritual, but extends to the most practical forms of assistance in times of trouble, in getting jobs, and in helping to start businesses. Evangelical religion becomes the basis of "mediating institutions" that stand between the lone individual and the vast megastructures of society. The convert is embraced within a network of mutual assistance, constantly reinforced by prayer, Bible study, and ritual recommitment to the "fellowship of the saved." This is certainly not everything that the Church means by "communion and solidarity," but it is a communion and solidarity for which many feel a desperate need.

Of most particular importance in these evangelical movements is the role of women. This factor received hardly a mention at the synod. The importance is not in the fact that women assume positions of leadership, although that too sometimes happens. The importance, rather, is in providing women and their children a new security and respect. If there is anything antithetical to the evangelical ethos, it is the Latin culture of *machismo*. Conversion is conversion from philandering, drunkenness, drugs, and indolence. Little wonder that the evangelical insurgency is so largely driven by women. They are not "feminists" in the North American sense of the term that so concerned some of the Canadian bishops. It is not a matter of women wanting to take over. On the contrary, the determination of these women is to have their men assume their responsibilities as men. Evangelicalism might be described as a women's movement to get men moving. Needless to say, there is a direct connection between a family improving its economic condition and men who are faithful, responsible, sober, and hard-working. In short, evangelical Protestantism presents itself as offering not only a more authentic encounter with Christ but also a more sure way of getting ahead in the world. Getting ahead in the world is, in turn, often seen as confirmation of a saving encounter with Christ. Here too there is an echo of Max Weber's proposed connection between capitalism and the Protestant ethic.

Evangelicalism, then, is an indigenous and permanent fact of life in Latin America. It is a cultural fact at the deepest level of culture, which is religious. And it is a religio-cultural fact of economic and political significance, in terms both of its sources and of its consequences. The economic, political, and cultural are tightly entangled in one package, but the Church's attention must be on the priority of the cultural. It is in the realm of culture that it has its chief authority, competence, and potential influence. The purpose must not be to maintain

an intact "Catholic culture" in a monopolistic sense of that term. Pluralism is written into the script of history, and that will become ever
more evident also in Latin America. The effort to maintain a Catholic
monopoly can only provoke equally monopolistic counterefforts. Historically, this is what happened in countries such as Uruguay. Catholic
monopoly is challenged and displaced by anti-Catholic secularism that
captures state power. Today, some in Latin America see "the sects"
replacing Enlightenment rationalism and Freemasonry as the enemy
of Catholic culture. But that entire way of thinking is riddled through
and through with the disease of monism.

Monism insists that it must be all or nothing, all one way or all the
other. Pluralism recognizes that, short of the final consummation of
the kingdom of God, history is a mixed bag. Vatican II teaches that the
Church is the "sacrament" of that promised future of the kingdom. A
sacrament is not engaged in the power politics of forcing history, but
can only believably and persuasively signify a promise of what might
be. Does this mean that there is not a real contest and competition
between the Church and the evangelical movements? No, contest and
competition are inevitable, especially as these movements define
themselves in hostility to the Church. But here *Lumen Gentium* not only
is the correct theology but also suggests the wisest strategy. Insofar as
the Church makes it unquestionably clear that it views these other
Christians as brothers and sisters in Christ, it also disarms them. To the
extent, on the other hand, that they can successfully depict the Church
as the *ancien régime* of hierarchical power seeking and monopolistic
control over society, the evangelical movements can present themselves
as the courageous resistance, even as martyrs to truth and freedom.

The Church Imposes Nothing

As we have seen, the Synod for America was, for the most part, a synod
for Latin America. This was evident both in the balance of representation and in the issues most urgently addressed. Economic issues, such
as international debts, received much attention, but always within the
context of trying to redefine the relationship between the North and
South. Whether bishops spoke about "invasion" or "corruption" from

the North, always the great fear is that Latin America is being taken over by the North, and, more specifically, by the United States. This is nothing new, for that fear has dominated relations between South and North almost from the beginning. It has largely defined the political relationship between the states of the two regions. Throughout the synod, one sensed a yearning to break out of that old pattern, a hope that the Church *as Church* might be able to establish a new and more constructive relationship between South and North.

In the formal and informal discussions, there was a persistent swinging back and forth between bishops speaking as representatives of regional and national interests and speaking as bishops of the one Church. This is inevitable, for all of us are implicated in several communities and the identities attached to those communities. It is only as members of the Church, however, that we know a community that truly encompasses "America" in the singular. Listening to some Latin American interventions, one was regularly reminded of the maxim mentioned earlier: "All our problems are the result of massive American intervention. The solution to all our problems is massive American intervention." That of course is the old language of dependency, and it never sounds so poignantly dependent as when it is employed in angry protest against the hegemony of the North. But just as often Latin Americans spoke in a new and more promising way. Not content to rail against "neoliberalism" and "globalization" and other imperialist monsters, they engaged in serious self-examination about what it means to be the Catholic Church in Latin America. Nor were the North Americans passive observers in this process. They were manifestly eager to help, and just as eager not to seem patronizing in their eagerness to help. Some of the North American talk about "receiving more than we give" in the relationship with the South was no doubt politeness. But joined to it was a deep and justified uneasiness about what the U.S. hegemony means for the rest of the world, and about the ineffectiveness of the Church in influencing that hegemony.

What was new and promising became most evident when bishops left off from talking about the Church as an agent of political or economic change and concentrated attention on the Church *as Church*. For all the appurtenances of power it has acquired at different times and in different ways, the Church is finally the community of a crucified Lord. This is not to say that the Church does not hold to firm

truths that impinge also upon the political and economic power realities of the world. She has a strong and elaborate tradition of social
teaching, but she does not have and should not want the power to
impose that teaching on the world. John Paul II says in *Redemptoris Missio*, "The Church imposes nothing. She only proposes." With respect to
the right ordering of a free and just society, the Church has many proposals to make and nowhere are they brought together so comprehensively and persuasively as in the 1991 encyclical *Centesimus Annus*.

With most specific reference to the post-communist societies of
Central and Eastern Europe, but with an applicability that is universal,
Centesimus Annus makes clear that the days of the "power Church" are
past. She imposes nothing; she only proposes. She would not impose if
she could. Her sphere is the cultural, and she gladly accepts that, believing confidently in the priority of culture. She knows that in the sphere
of the cultural there are many counterproposals. They are not to be
squelched by power but are to be engaged by respectful dialogue. The
Church is not intimidated by pluralism, for pluralism is the inevitable
consequence of freedom, and the Church is the world's premier champion of freedom. This fearlessness in the face of differences that make
the greatest difference is most crucially tested in encounters at the heart
of culture, which is religion. And that is why the most important question addressed by the synod is the encounter with other Christians. For
Latin Americans it is a matter of positioning the Church for an
encounter that is still relatively new. For North Americans, it is a matter
of reexamining the ways in which a very old encounter has confused or
compromised what it means to be a Catholic Christian.

Freedom Is Not the Enemy of Truth

We are returned to the wry comment of the bishop who says that
maybe Latin America is not ready for *Lumen Gentium*. Maybe that is
just as true of North America. Or maybe what this synod revealed is
that only now are both North and South in a position to act on the challenge and promise of *Lumen Gentium*. In a pluralistic world, sur-
rounded by other churches and religious communities, what does it
mean to be the Catholic Church? In North America, and especially in

the United States, Catholicism was, for the most part, a latecomer to a country already in secure Protestant possession. In Latin America, Catholicism was "present at the creation." The Church gave cultural and political definition to what it means to be Latin American. No part of the Latin American "identity kit" is untouched by Catholicism. In the North, the great task was to prove that Catholicism really belonged, that it did not threaten the social order, that Catholics could succeed in being "good Americans"—as their Protestant neighbors defined what it means to be a good American. The success of Catholics in passing that test is nothing short of astonishing. Now, as Francis George and others have reminded the synod, the question for North Americans is whether they are good Catholics.

In the North, the Church is tempted by cultural accommodation. One might at first think that is not the case in the South. After all, how can accommodating to a "Catholic culture" be viewed as a temptation? But it is worth asking whether cultural accommodation is not the crisis for the Church in both North and South. In this context, cultural accommodation means making an idol of the culture; it means subordinating the Church's self-understanding to other definitions of reality; it means becoming, in the words of Jesus, salt that has lost its savor. The cultural captivity of the Church takes different forms. In the North, it is viewed as liberal and progressive when the Church demonstrates that it poses no threat to the regnant culture. In the South, it is viewed as conservative and reactionary when the Church is identified with a culture threatened by change. Both are cultural captivities unworthy of the Church described by *Lumen Gentium*. In neither case is the Church being faithful to her self-understanding as the sacrament of the One who is *Lumen Gentium*—Christ, the light of the nations.

The Church in the North is often marked by timidity, an eagerness not to offend those who are not Catholic. It may seem to be the opposite in the South when the Church aggressively opposes those who are not Catholic. But that too is a form of timidity, a fear of critically engaging "others." Critical engagement is the course of confident faith that everything that is good and true and beautiful outside the Church gravitates toward unity with the Church. In the words of *Lumen Gentium*, these realities "possess an inner dynamism toward Catholic unity." It is worth recalling the crucial passage:

This Church, constituted and organized in the world as a society, sub-
sists in the Catholic Church, which is governed by the successor of Peter
and by the bishops in union with that successor, although many elements of sanctification and of truth can be found outside her visible
structure. These elements, however, as gifts properly belonging to the
Church of Christ, possess an inner dynamism toward Catholic unity.

It may seem unspeakably arrogant to claim that all elements of
sanctification and truth gravitate toward the Catholic Church because
they gravitate toward Christ, and it is arrogant if it is not true. But
Catholics believe it is true. And there is no room for arrogance when
we recall that, while these elements belong to the Church, they are ours
only as "gifts." Again, *Lumen Gentium* puts the matter very nicely when
it says that Catholics should ever be mindful that "they owe their distinguished status not to their own merits, but to Christ's special grace;
and if they fail to respond to this grace in thought, word, and deed, not
only will they not be saved, they will be judged more severely." In relating to other Christians, says *Ut Unum Sint*, we must present the fullness
of the truth.

At the same time, [the council] asks that the manner and method of
expounding the Catholic faith should not be a hindrance to dialogue
with our brothers and sisters. Certainly it is possible to profess one's
faith and to explain its teaching in a way that is correct, fair, and understandable, and which at the same time takes into account both the way
of thinking and the actual historical experiences of the other party.

The New Thing in Latin America

Whether in the North or the South, that "way of thinking and actual
historical experience" leads many Christians to view the Catholic
Church with suspicion and hostility. Suspicion and hostility can be
overcome by superficial accommodation, by pretending that our differences make no real difference, but that is to betray the truth. The
truth is that there are very big differences and that they make a very
real difference. Yet the truth is not the obstacle to overcoming suspicion and hostility. On the contrary, it is the only way to do so. The
truth is that—however imperfect our communion, however deep our

mutual suspicion and hostility—we are brothers and sisters in Christ. Recognizing that fact is not optional. It is the fact established by the grace of God. To paraphrase *Lumen Gentium*, if we fail to respond to the grace in others, which is the same grace by which we are saved, we invoke God's judgment upon ourselves.

If we are right in believing in the priority of culture, and that at the heart of culture is cult, then this ecumenical engagement is the most critical question addressed by the Synod for America. In the North, what is called ecumenism has too often been a matter of mere social accommodation. A great gift from the South to the North would be to demonstrate an authentic ecumenism that is radically grounded in Christ and his saving gospel, an ecumenism thoroughly "inculturated" in a Latin American way of being confidently Catholic enough to welcome, and not to fear, the pluralism that will certainly shape the future.

Such pluralism is not to be viewed as an import from the North, as an appendix to economic, social, political, and other threatening changes. Rather, pluralism engaged at its heart—which is to say at the point of *religious* pluralism—is the fulcrum by which the entire society can be transformed. The Catholic Church is the only cultural institution in a position to work this change. The task is daunting, but not impossible. In Latin American countries, the result will certainly change what has been meant by Catholic culture. But that is already changing in any event. The question is whether the Catholic Church will be in a perpetually defensive posture, desperately trying against all odds to preserve its cultural monopoly, or will dare to act on the claim of *Lumen Gentium* that it is the Church of Jesus Christ most fully and rightly ordered through time, and therefore has nothing to fear.

If this happens in Latin America, it would be something quite new. It is emphatically not a case of replicating the experience of the North. In the North, Catholics were immigrant outsiders and thought they had everything to gain by accommodating themselves to a non-Catholic culture. In the South, Catholics had, or thought they had, a cultural monopoly, and it would appear that there is much to lose in a pluralistic future. Much will be lost if that pluralistic future is forced upon the Church in Latin America. Much will be gained, however, if it is imaginatively shaped by the Church in generous cooperation with other Christians with whom common cause can be made against cul-

tural forces that are hostile to Christianity itself. Of course these other
Christians are, more often than not, hostile to the Catholic Church. In
many cases, that hostility seems to be the very core of their identity, the
motor force of their propaganda and proselytizing passion. By recip-
rocating that hostility, the Church can only deepen that identity,
increase the credibility of that propaganda, and further inflame that
proselytizing passion. Many leaders of these new movements count on
the Church's relentless hostility. The Church should not play into their
hands.

Healing the Breaches

Again, there is no room for naiveté in thinking about this pluralistic
future. It will in many instances involve painful dislocations and will be
accompanied by social and economic changes over which the Church
has very limited control. What the Church can influence, if not control, is the cultural consequence of a transformation that is, whether
we like it or not, already under way. This depends on leadership that is
not merely reactive but boldly anticipates a different future. From
Medellin onward, the Church in Latin America embarked upon a positive pastoral strategy, recognizing that the "cultural Catholicism" of
the past was in many ways a delusion. That pastoral strategy was for a
time hijacked by the Marxist distraction championed by some liberation theologies. Now largely freed from that distraction, the synod
called the Church back to the core pastoral tasks of evangelization, catechesis, care for the marginal, priestly vocations, and the direction of
an astonishing variety of lay movements of radical discipleship. In a
new circumstance of cultural and religious pluralism—a circumstance
that is not of the Church's choosing—ecumenism is a necessary component of all these tasks.

In many places in Latin America there is little or no real experience with ecumenism. In other places there is long-standing cooperation with the very tame "oldline" groups such as Lutherans, Anglicans,
or Methodists, but no constructive encounter with evangelicals and
pentecostalists, who are the real challenge. The beginnings of serious
ecumenical engagement will necessarily be hesitant and uncertain, and

there will no doubt be rebuffs and setbacks. Many evangelical entrepreneurs are building their religious empires and have a steep investment in the Catholic Church remaining the enemy. With the patience that is born of confidence, Catholics must keep their eyes on the goal, which is that in the twenty-first century Catholics and evangelicals will reevangelize Latin America with one another rather than against one another. If it is clearly seen that Catholics took the lead in bringing about this change, the result may also be a renewed and strengthened Catholic culture in the countries of Latin America. Catholic culture will be renewed because it will have demonstrated its ability to anticipate, and not merely react to, historical change. And it will be strengthened because it will no longer be seen as the oppressive burden of centuries past but as the thoroughly inculturated achievement of the Latin America of the twenty-first century.

All the evidence suggests that John Courtney Murray was right: Pluralism is written into the script of history. Pluralism is the social name of freedom. The Church is the sacramental sign that points to and now anticipates the promised time when freedom is perfectly joined to truth. That time is not yet. Along the way to the kingdom, the Church must by word and holiness of life contend, persuade, explain, exhort, and entreat on behalf of the truth. She fears no encounters. She engages others in the sure confidence that—however circuitous and difficult the route—everything good, true, and beautiful gravitates toward unity with the Church because everything good, true, and beautiful gravitates toward unity with the Church's Lord. Between East and West, between North and South, between Protestant and Catholic, all the breaches will be healed, and the prayer, *ut unum sint,* will be answered. In God's time and God's way, which is just as it should be.

The Church's way through history is the way of freedom. She knows that human freedom can be abused, exploited, and sometimes turned against the truth. But she will never accept that freedom is the enemy of truth, for it is the truth that makes us free. Within the community of the Church, we remind ourselves that truth needs no protection from freedom, even as we persuade those outside the Church that their freedom needs no protection from the truth. Faith in this ultimately unbreakable bond between freedom and truth makes it possible for *Redemptoris Missio* to declare, "The Church imposes nothing. She only proposes." But what a proposal!

7

Ready or Not, the Third Millennium

Springtime for a Church and a World Ever Young

I CANNOT TAKE BACK what I said at the start about the tedium of the Synod for America. Nor would I withdraw the suggestion—seconded, I know, by many bishops—that somebody should take a long and critical look at the way these synods are structured. So much time, so much money, and so much talent are deserving of a process that lends itself to orderly deliberation of the questions on which the Holy Father desires the counsel of the synod. That having been said, however, and having now tried to pull together the many disconnected interventions and conversations of these weeks, I am impressed by how much happened.

The synod provided a kind of snapshot of the Church's leadership at the end of the twentieth century, or at least of the leadership of the Church that includes half of the more than one billion Catholic Christians in the world. It is not necessarily the most accurate snapshot. For a different snapshot, we would have to go to the local churches on the ground, so to speak—to places such as Chicago, Miami, Montreal, Caracas, Lima, Santiago, and Kingston. Even better, we would need a first-hand familiarity with the thousands of parishes, base communities, and lay movements that *are* the Church in America. As assembling bishops in a national episcopal conference creates dynamics different from those same bishops working in their local churches, so a further step removed from the basic reality of the Church is a synod that

150

brings together in an unprecedented way the bishops of "America" in the singular—"from Alaska to Tierra del Fuego."

What has Port-au-Prince in common with Kansas City, or San Salvador with Winnipeg? To ask the question is to point to another sense in which the Synod for America, far from being a distorting abstraction from the reality of the Church on the ground, focuses attention on the core reality of what it means to be the Catholic Church. The synod is—above all and through and through—a papal event. It is, quite simply, a gathering of the successors of the apostles around the successor of Peter. That ecclesial and theological definition is the only thing that can make sense of what happened here, and of what will come of it. The synod was proposed by the pope, convened by the pope, presided over by the pope, and the pope will deliver the official statement of what it achieved. But always it is Peter in consultation with the other apostles, just as the Second Vatican Council intended when it spoke of collegiality.

This is qualitatively different from a corporate CEO meeting with his top management. The pope is not at the top of a pyramid but at the center of a community. The meaning of the synod does not trickle down from the top but radiates out from the center. And always at the very epicenter of the center is Christ, the one whose words are lettered six feet high round the dome of St. Peter's basilica: *Tu es Petrus, et super hanc petram aedificabo ecclesiam meam et tibi dabo claves regni coelorum.* The formal prayers at the synod take up but a small part of the time devoted to speeches, discussions, and the drafting and redrafting of documents. Yet to neglect the prayer is to miss the point of the entire exercise. Peter and the other apostles are gathered to ask, "What would he have us do?" The question is asked in the expectation of an answer, for he said, "When the Spirit of truth comes, he will guide you into all the truth" (John 16:13). It might be objected that this is an impossibly "idealistic" reading of an event such as this synod, and it certainly can be read in other ways—in terms of management studies, sociology, or even politics. Those and other factors are engaged, of course, but the impossibly idealistic reading is the only possible reading if we are to make sense of what happened here, even if all of us who were participants were not always aware of that.

A Synod of Vatican Council II

The idea of this apostolic consultation—and of the other continental synods for Africa, Europe, Asia, and Oceania—was born from a sense of heightened expectation surrounding the third Christian millennium. It is well known that when Karol Wojtyla was elected pope, Stefan Cardinal Wyszynski, then primate of Poland, told him he had been elected to lead the Church into the third millennium. John Paul has referred publicly to that prophetic word of Wyszynski, and it is almost impossible to exaggerate the degree to which this heightened expectation, an expectation that some call "mystical," has formed his pontificate. In his 1994 apostolic letter *Tertio Millennio Adveniente* ("As the Third Millennium Nears"), he writes:

> In fact, preparing for the year 2000 has become as it were a hermeneutical key of my pontificate. It is certainly not a matter of indulging in a new millenarianism, as occurred in some quarters at the end of the first millennium; rather, it is aimed at an increased sensitivity to all that the Spirit is saying to the Church and to the churches (see Revelation 2:7ff.).

For the pope, this heightened expectation or increased sensitivity is not just the hermeneutical or interpretive key of his own pontificate. It is the key to the recent history of the Church. As one who is emphatically "a man of the council," he sees the past thirty and more years as a *kairos*—a moment of providential opportunity. In the same letter, he notes that the Second Vatican Council is often viewed "as the beginning of a new era in the life of the Church." Keeping faith with the past, the council and the popes since the council have tried to put the Church on full alert to the new thing that God may be doing. This entire period should be viewed as a "preparation of that new springtime of Christian life which will be revealed by the Great Jubilee if Christians are responsive to the action of the Holy Spirit."

The preparation of that hoped-for springtime, of which the Synod for America is part, is undertaken against an eschatological horizon. The subject of eschatology may seem to have more to do with autumn and winter than with springtime, for it ordinarily deals with the end of history and Christ's return to judge the living and the dead. But in *Tertio Millennio Adveniente*, endings and beginnings are joined in the mystery of Christ. By virtue of what happened two thousand years ago in Bethlehem,

> The world of creatures appears as a "cosmos," an ordered universe. And it is the same Word who, by taking flesh, renews the cosmic order of creation. The Letter to the Ephesians speaks of the purpose which God had set forth in Christ, "as a plan for the fullness of time, to unite all things in him, things in heaven and things on earth."

Springtime is the appropriate image. We might say the world is getting not older but younger, for the Word of God through whom all things came to be and in whom all things cohere is ever young. In his compellingly personal meditation, *Crossing the Threshold of Hope,* John Paul lifts up the cosmic dimension of this springtime. "It can be said that until recently the Church's catechesis and preaching centered upon an *individual eschatology,* one, for that matter, which is profoundly rooted in divine revelation. The vision proposed by the council, however, what that of an *eschatology of the Church and of the world.*" For the Church and for the world, it is springtime because "Christ is ever young." We have seen how in the course of the synod attention was turned again and again to young people, with frequent reference to their remarkable response to John Paul.

The pope explains this in terms of a perpetual springtime of joy and love. In *Threshold* he writes:

> *As a young priest I learned to love human love.* This has been one of the fundamental themes of my priesthood. . . . If one loves human love, there naturally arises the need to commit oneself completely to the service of "fair love," because love is fair, it is beautiful.

Even if young people sometimes give in to weakness and their passions become ugly, "in the depths of their hearts they still desire a beautiful and pure love."

> We need the enthusiasm of the young. We need their *joie de vivre.* In it is reflected something of the original joy God had in creating man. . . . It is not true that the Pope brings the young from one end of the world to the other. It is they who bring him. Even though he is getting older, they urge him to be young, they do not permit him to forget his experience, his discovery of youth and its great importance for the life of every man.

This Pope "Has No Pride"

This Christ-centered intuition of a vibrantly young world living in "the fullness of time" permeates the message of *Tertio Millennio Adveniente*. Nor is it entirely absent from the *Nuntius,* or "Message to America" issued by the synod fathers. Indeed, the opening passage of that message reads:

> At the threshold of the third millennium of Christianity, the members of the Special Assembly of the Synod of Bishops for America call out to all our brothers and sisters in America, and to all the world, the words which St. Paul proclaimed at the beginning of the first millennium, "Jesus Christ is Lord!"

The message lists the "joys" and "concerns" of the Church in America, with more than four times as much space given to the concerns. While the new evangelization calls for assertiveness in creating a new culture of life, the synod's message is preoccupied with the "new culture" being created by the communications media and "aggressive secularism." It calls on others "to stand with us against anti-religious prejudice and to support the contributions of the Church and other communities of faith to the common good." The note of eschatological confidence is not missing: "Do not be afraid to cross the threshold of hope. There we shall all meet the Lord, the living Jesus Christ, who is our hope and our salvation." But the reader of "Message to America" might be forgiven for coming away from it with the feeling that the Church is besieged, on the defensive, and generally overwhelmed by forces antagonistic to the promised springtime.

Strikingly absent from the synod message is an accent on Christian unity. Fortunately, that question figures prominently in the synod's final propositions submitted to the Holy Father. In its summary of the final propositions *Origins*, published by Catholic News Service, reports:

> The synod stressed ecumenism's essential role in the new evangelization. And while deploring aggressive proselytizing by non-Catholic religious movements, especially in traditionally Catholic regions, the synod distinguished evangelical Christian churches, with whose members Catholics share the grace of baptism, from religious sects or cults. They said that in response to the proselytizing activities of new religious movements the Church should renew its pastoral methods and offer

more personal attention to the faithful, more effective preaching, and more meditation on Scripture.

On this score the propositions are in tune with *Tertio Millennio*, which, we recall, sets out the vision that this and the other continental synods are to advance. There the pope wrote:

> Among the most fervent petitions which the Church makes to the Lord during this important time, as the eve of the new millennium approaches, is that unity among all Christians of the various confessions will increase until they reach full communion. I pray that the jubilee will be a promising opportunity for fruitful cooperation in the many areas which unite us; these are unquestionably more numerous than those which divide us.

In the same letter, John Paul expresses the hope that other churches and communities will join in developing programs to prepare for the jubilee. Shortly after the letter was issued in 1994, the World Council of Churches, which includes most of the oldline "ecumenical" churches, declined the invitation, rather sniffily observing that they had not been included in the initial planning. The evangelical and pentecostal groups that have not been part of the ecumenical movement are far from ready for formal cooperation with the Catholic Church, and we have already noted the difficult relationship with the Orthodox. And so it appears that whatever world Christianity will be doing in a programmatic way to observe the third Christian millennium will be mainly up to the Catholic Church.

Undaunted, the pope presses ahead and urges the Church to do likewise. This is a characteristic of the Holy Father that some in the Curia call stubbornness; he never takes no for an answer; he refuses to be rebuffed by rebuffs. In the search for Christian unity, in the planning for the millennium, in his effort to heal wounds between Christians and Jews, and on much else, when his invitations are declined, his proposals are spurned, and his gestures of good will go unreciprocated, he is undeterred. He simply keeps coming back to try again. "He has no pride," a curial cardinal tells me, and he means that as a compliment. "He knows what has to be done and, if there is no positive response today, maybe there will be a better response tomorrow. He is not going to be discouraged in making the record of this pontificate clear. If what he suggests doesn't happen today, he looks to history and, finally, to God for vindication. Almost everything he is doing now is sowing seeds for the future. He is very patient."

Healing Memories

Few proposals of this pope have met with such resistance from within the Curia and the college of cardinals as his insistence that the Church must undergo a "healing of memories" in preparing for the third millennium. Nonetheless, he made this a central theme of *Tertio Millennio*. The Church must cross the threshold on her knees if she is to stand upright in the next millennium.

> Hence it is appropriate that as the second millennium of Christianity draws to a close the Church should become more fully conscious of the sinfulness of her children, recalling all those times in history when they departed from the spirit of Christ and his gospel and, instead of offering to the world the witness of a life inspired by the values of faith, indulged in ways of thinking and acting which were truly forms of counter witness and scandal.

The objection was, to put it simply, that the pope was opening a can of worms. Rummaging through history to find and publicly expose Catholic failings, it was said, could only have the result of putting the Church on the defensive. It would result in the Church being perceived as crossing the millennial threshold not so much in penitence as in an apologetic mode, and the enemies of the Church would never be satisfied with any apology. The grievances are so massive and various, it was said, that nothing would be accepted as sufficient until the Church apologizes for her very existence. This also touches on the critical theological distinction between the sinfulness of the Church's members and the sinfulness of the Church herself. Because she is the Body of Christ and because the premier icon of the Church is the sinless Virgin Mary, it is not theologically possible to say that the Church has sinned, and yet such fine distinctions will certainly be lost in the media's treatment of any apologies or statements of penitence issuing from Rome. Such were among the objections to the pope's proposal.

On the distinction between the Church and her members, *Tertio Millennio* put the matter this way:

> Although she is holy because of her incorporation into Christ, the Church does not tire of doing penance: Before God and man she always acknowledges as her own her sinful sons and daughters. As *Lumen Gentium* affirms: "The Church, embracing sinners to her bosom, is at the same time holy and always in need of being purified, and incessantly pursues the paths of penance and renewal."

It is not simply a matter of saying that mistakes were sometimes made. John Paul is uncompromising: "Another painful chapter of history to which the sons and daughters of the Church must return with a spirit of repentance is that of the acquiescence given, especially in certain centuries, to intolerance and even the use of violence in the service of truth."

The pope allows that history is ambiguous and people were caught up in complex circumstances that may make their sinful actions understandable, but that cannot be pleaded as an excuse.

> Yet the consideration of mitigating factors does not exonerate the Church from the obligation to express profound regret for the weaknesses of so many of her sons and daughters who sullied her face, preventing her from fully mirroring the image of her crucified Lord, the supreme witness of patient love and of humble meekness.

The radical thinking of this pope—a radicality that some believe is naiveté—leads him to believe that "patient love" and "humble meekness" can be communicated and understood in a contemporary culture that appears to know only the categories of power and weakness. In response to that criticism one must ask, What image should the Church represent to the world other than that of her crucified Lord? Of course it is a high-risk enterprise. It was that two thousand years ago.

No Apology for Being Catholic

One of the most distinguished auditors at the Synod for America was Mary Ann Glendon, professor of law at Harvard. Shortly before the synod convened, she published in the November 1997 issue of *First Things* an article that turned out to be prescient, "Contrition in the Age of Spin Control." The public confession of sins takes on new perils, she said, when "historians seem increasingly to have turned from the search for fact toward freewheeling, imaginative reconstructions of events." "As for the popular image of the Church in history," she wrote, "it must be hard for Catholics brought up on movies and TV to avoid the impression that their Church holds a special niche in some historical hall of shame. Add to this that most people hear of official expressions of regret as filtered through the news media." Glendon is fully supportive of the pope's intention in *Tertio Millennio,* but notes that "though the Pope himself is careful to speak of sin or error on the part of the Church's members or representatives, rather than the Church in its fullness, that important theological distinction is almost always lost in the transmission."

She cites an article in which the dissident German theologian Hans Küng is dismissive of the pope's many statements about the failures of Catholics during the Holocaust. For Küng, she says, no confession will do until the pope endorses the bizarre view that "it is no longer possible to say the Nazis were responsible without saying the Church is co-responsible." Shortly after the Synod for America, the Vatican issued a long-awaited statement, "We Remember: Reflections on the Shoah." Professor Glendon's worst fears were realized when it was met with a chorus of criticism, mainly from Jewish sources, declaring the statement to be "hollow," "not enough," and "too little too late." The statement was most stridently attacked for its failure to pronounce an outright condemnation of Pope Pius XII and his alleged silence and indifference during the Holocaust (an allegation that is, as "We Remember" and many scholarly works make clear, contrary to fact).

Public expressions of contrition, says Glendon, "are being opportunistically exploited by persons or groups who are only too eager to help the Church rend her garments and to heap more ashes on the heads of Catholics." When we ask forgiveness, she observes, we are addressing ourselves first and foremost to God. "Expressions of sorrow over past shortcomings do not require abasing ourselves before others, and certainly not before persons who are unwilling to admit any misdeed of their own. Many historical memories will not be healed until there has been mutual forgiveness." The Holy Father has said there must be public acts of repentance, and so there must. But, Glendon writes, "Let us make sure our expressions of sorrow are never permitted to denigrate the role of the Church in history as an overwhelmingly positive force for peace and justice. And, above all, let us remember what they are not: they are not apologies for being Catholic."

The Latin American Difference

We saw that at the opening Mass for the Synod for America, the pope strongly affirmed the first evangelization of America five hundred years ago. In this he was deliberately defying the fashionably revisionist accounts of "1492 and all that," which depict it as an instance of brutal conquest and imperialist despoliation. In the course of the synod itself, there were many statements of regret—one might even call them confessions—over the treatment of indigenous peoples, and the general secretary of the U.S. bishops' conference even managed to suggest that the United States should apologize to the millions of immigrants who believed they were coming to the land of opportunity. Yet it is not evident that these and other statements qualified as the acts of penitence called for by *Tertio Millennio*. They were more reflective of the regnant pattern of feeling guilty that is today cultivated among white people of European extraction, or at least among those of a certain educational and cultural attainment. Of course that phenomenon is not found among bishops of Latin America and the Caribbean, who tend to be, in the jargon of North Americans, "people of color."

The penitential theme of *Tertio Millennio* is different from the synod also in another respect. Many of the confessions at the synod were offered on behalf of the cultures or countries of which the bishops are part, not on behalf of Catholics as such. That generalization needs to be qualified by several distinctions. The Canadians, for instance, did not seem to be confessing Catholic failures, nor to be confessing on behalf of their culture. Theirs were statements less of confession than of complaint. They vehemently complained about a culture that they viewed as hostile, and there was at least a suggestion that the Church's magisterium is guilty of holding to positions that are responsible for marginalizing the Church in Canada. Apart from allusions to the ill-treatment of Indians, and an acknowledgment that more must be done for immigrants from the South, the U.S. bishops, too, provided no acts of penitence. At the same time, being keenly aware of their position of relative strength and wealth, the Americans were at pains not to appear overbearing. They exhibited a generally inoffensive mix of deference and noblesse oblige.

With the Latin Americans it was different. Coming from cultures that are in some serious sense Catholic, the line between cultural confession and Catholic confession is not so clear. Going back over the many interventions and conversations, however, I am impressed that the bishops from the South were inclined to be more self-critical than those from the North. The Canadians blamed their culture and (at least implicitly) Rome for their problems, while the Americans, it is fair to say, did not seem to have many problems, at least not really big ones. The Latin Americans, on the other hand, acknowledged a host of problems. While much was blamed on the North and on forces such as "the sects," "neoliberalism," and "globalization," the Latin American bishops candidly acknowledged historic failures in their own spheres of responsibility, notably in evangelization, catechesis, preaching, and pastoral care. They came closest, I believe, to the self-examination and contrition that the Holy Father called for in *Tertio Millennio*.

The "American Experiment" Threatened

The pope himself has some very definite views about the self-examination that is in order for the people of the United States, including Catholics and their bishops. On December 16, four days after the closing of the synod, and making specific reference to the synod, John Paul reflected on "the American experiment." The occasion was his receiving the credentials of Corinne (Lindy) Boggs as the new U.S. ambassador to the Holy See. He noted that the founding fathers affirmed "self-evident" truths about the human person which can be discerned by reason and have their ground in "nature and nature's God." They understood that "freedom [is] designed to enable people to fulfill their duties and responsibilities toward the family and toward the common good of the community." He allowed that "the American democratic experiment has been successful in many ways. Millions of people around the world look to the United States as a model in their search for freedom, dignity, and prosperity." Particularly impressive is America's devotion to human rights and "to the fundamental human right of religious freedom, which is the guarantee of every other human right." But he cautioned that the experiment so nobly launched cannot be sustained "without a deeply rooted vision of divine providence over the individual and over the fate of nations."

Then the pope turned explicitly to the theme of *Tertio Millennio*, and what he said bears close reading:

As the year 2000 draws near and Christians prepare to celebrate the bi-millennium of the birth of Christ, I have appealed for a serious examination of conscience regarding the shadows that darken our times. Nations and states too can make this a time of reflection on the spiritual and moral conditions of their success in promoting the integral good of their people. It would truly be a sad thing if the religious and moral convictions upon which the American experiment was founded could now somehow be considered a danger to free society, such that those who would bring these convictions to bear upon your nation's public life would be denied a voice in debating and resolving issues of public policy. The original separation of church and state in the United States was certainly not an effort to ban all religious conviction from the public sphere, a kind of banishment of God from civil society. Indeed, the vast majority of Americans, regardless of their religious persuasion, are convinced that religious conviction and religiously informed moral argument have a vital role in public life.

Very specifically, John Paul alluded to the dangers when certain members of the human community—the unborn, the old, the sick, the radically handicapped—are excluded from the protection of law. When that happens, "a deadly anarchy subverts the original understanding of justice." "The credibility of the United States will depend more and more on its promotion of a genuine culture of life, and on a renewed commitment to building a world in which the weakest and most vulnerable are welcomed and protected." He noted that the Synod for America had highlighted the many ways in which the Catholics of the United States contribute to the common good, and he offered a prayer "that your country will experience a new birth of freedom, freedom grounded in truth and ordered to goodness."

It was gracious of the pope to mention the synod in this connection, but it must be admitted that no American bishops there gave voice to his sense of the promise, also for the world, of the American experiment, or of the great dangers overtaking that experiment. Perhaps that can be explained by a misplaced sense of humility and the desire of most Americans to maintain a low profile. Or maybe bishops feel they have enough to do in worrying about more specifically ecclesiastical problems. I am impressed also by the synod's apparently lukewarm response to the suggestion that "the culture of life," a theme so close to the heart of the pope, should be a driving passion informing the future of the Church in the Americas. But again, maybe the response wasn't lukewarm. Maybe it is simply that the importance of the culture of life is taken for granted. It goes without saying, we may think, until it is recalled that things do not really go unless they are said.

A *Company of Good Cheer*

The Synod for America, like the other continental synods, is part of the encompassing vision set forth in *Tertio Millennio Adveniente*. There were moments that brought alive the searching self-examination and heightened expectation that the apostolic letter calls for. But, it must honestly be said, only moments. To expect more from a synod of bishops is perhaps to expect too much. Bishops, as a rule, are not visionaries. It is no little thing to faithfully carry on—to teach, to rule, to sanctify, and try to hold together communities of faith in which holiness can happen. Time and again during those long days in the aula, in meeting rooms, in the chapel, over dinner, wherever, I was caught up short by the thought that here are men who, with few exceptions, have no delusions about being in control. They are not their own men.

My friend said of them that they don't know anything other than the Church. That can be limiting, no doubt, but I expect it is not untouched by what Jesus meant when he spoke about losing our lives in order to find our lives. They understand, and most seem to be at peace with the understanding, that they are servants of something immeasurably grander than themselves: the One, Holy, Catholic, and Apostolic Church. Titles, robes, insignia, and gestures of deference notwithstanding, few betray the strut of self-importance. All in all, they know that this Catholic thing is in no way their own invention; it has been going for centuries and will endure until Our Lord returns in glory. To be a bishop is to be a success of sorts, but it is nothing to be puffed up about: they know there were thousands of others before them and will be thousands after them. They pray that during their little moment on stage they will not play the fool or be found unfaithful.

There are few commanding figures among them; great minds are the exception, and the oratory is not for the ages. Many seem tired, worn, and a bit tattered around the edges, but it is, for all that, a cheerful company. And a company confident that somehow, in ways that elude clear discernment, they are instrumental to the fulfillment of a transcendent promise on which simply everything depends. They are and this synod was, in short, pretty much what one might expect had the original apostles, multiplied many times over, been sent to western shores and then, many years later, called back to Rome to consult with Peter. To consult, and to pray, and to repledge allegiances, and to hope against hope that they do not get in the way of the Holy Spirit bringing about something like an "Encounter with the Living Jesus Christ: The Way to Conversion, Communion, and Solidarity in America." Something like a springtime.

Index

Names

Subjects